Creative Mission

Published by
The Bible Reading Fellowship
15 The Chambers, Vineyard
Abingdon OX14 3FE
United Kingdom
Tel: +44 (0)1865 319700
Email: enquiries@brf.org.uk
Website: www.brf.org.uk
BRF is a Registered Charity

ISBN 978 1 84101 806 5

First published 2011
10 9 8 7 6 5 4 3 2 1 0

Acknowledgments
Unless otherwise stated, scripture quotations are taken from the Contemporary English Version of the Bible published by HarperCollins Publishers, copyright © 1991, 1992, 1995 American Bible Society.

Scripture quotations taken from the Holy Bible, New International Version, copyright © 1973, 1978, 1984 by International Bible Society, are used by permission of Hodder & Stoughton Publishers, a division of Hodder Headline Ltd. All rights reserved. 'NIV' is a registered trademark of International Bible Society. UK trademark number 1448790.

Scripture quotations from *The Message*. Copyright © by Eugene H. Peterson 1993, 1994, 1995. Used by permission of NavPress Publishing Group.

p. 80: Prisons Week prayer used by kind permission: www.prisonsweek.org
p. 99: Closing prayer taken from *The Promise of his Glory* by Church of England Liturgical Commission © Archbishops' Council. Used by permission.

A catalogue record for this book is available from the British Library

Printed in Singapore by Craft Print International Ltd

Creative Mission

Over 50 ideas for special days, celebrations, festivals, community-based projects and seasonal activities

Rona Orme

Acknowledgments

A book like this cannot be written without the ideas, help and encouragement of many people. In particular, I would like to thank:

Sue Doggett
Tim Sledge
Margaret Withers
The people of the Diocese of Peterborough

I first learned about mission at Polzeath, North Cornwall, from everyone involved in the Scripture Union beach mission. I dedicate this book to everyone who loves Polzeath, and to all who have served in mission there over so many years. I thank God for you all.

Now, I pray that the Holy Spirit will draw you to the ideas and possibilities that will work in your church and your community as you read this book. I find mission is fun—I hope you do too!

Contents

Mission ideas for Winter

Mission ideas for Spring

Mission ideas for Summer

Appendices

General index

*

Foreword

There have been plenty of books written about mission, outreach and children's work. Although they are important and enlightening, I have often been left with the question of how theory relates to practice. *Creative Mission* is a vital contribution to the church's ministry to children and families, thoroughly practical and wholly concerned with what we can actually do together as a church.

One of the distinctive contributions of this book is that while being rich and resourceful in its creativity, it is never light on theology and ecclesiology. There is a strong scriptural and liturgical strand running throughout, with activities for some saints and feast days that I don't think are covered anywhere else.

What I particularly like about this book is that it has a variety of activities, some starting from a festival or church base and others starting from the connections that children make within their own communities, which at present the church rarely makes the most of. Also, it never sells its soul to the temptation of entertainment. It is far more about presence, engagement and learning through play. I can see groups of children being thoroughly engrossed in the activities and hungry to learn more.

For every hardworking, often neglected but utterly precious children's worker, Sunday school leader and after-school club helper, this book is a treasury of ideas, resources and opportunities to help children grow in the joy of the gospel with others. This is the sort of book I will constantly be reaching for and using.

Creative Mission combines a heady cocktail of practical ideas, educational knowledge, theological grounding and engaging play. Drink deeply and quench your thirst for inspiration as the children in your church drink deeply of the beauty of the Christian faith.

The Revd Tim Sledge, Vicar of Romsey Abbey

*

Introduction

There are many families who have occasional contact with the church. They may have brought their child for baptism or thanksgiving. They may have chosen a church wedding. The children may attend a church-sponsored toddler group, nursery or pre-school, or a church school. They may attend a community school that occasionally visits the church for Religious Education (RE) lessons or carol services. The children may come to a service when they are being looked after by a grandparent. The families may just walk by and wonder what goes on inside.

This book contains a wide range of ideas to help churches, large and small, urban and rural, to work with the children and families who are unfamiliar with church life. Some ideas can be used within worship, both in church and in school assemblies. Other ideas are for social events, fundraising activities, lessons in citizenship and/or RE at school, and campaigns for justice across the world. All will appeal to children as well as adults, but many can also be used if there are few or no children in the church family.

Some of the ideas follow the Christian calendar. These suggest ways of sharing key moments in the liturgical year with the community or provide a wider range of special occasions to mark than exist in the secular calendar. The ideas are arranged in four sections to fit with the seasons of the year. This means that, occasionally, the Christian seasons do not fit comfortably into the printed calendar. The index will help you to find festivals and observances that do not link with a specific date.

Other suggestions provide ideas that link with secular high points in the year such as Valentine's Day, Red Nose Day, Father's Day and 'Back to School'. It is interesting to note that most of the main seasonal shopping opportunities, for which shops decorate with distinctive decorations, such as Christmas, Valentine's Day, Mother's Day, Easter and Hallowe'en, derive from Christian feasts and festivals.

Alongside these proposals, which are aimed at starting or developing a relationship between a church family and those with occasional contact, are suggestions for campaigning to improve life for children and families locally, nationally and across the world, and ideas to 'plant seeds' or to encourage the faith of children who only have a fleeting contact with a particular church. Some of these ideas are particularly good for churches that have few, or no, children in their congregation but who still wish to work with and for the next generation.

Not every church will feel able to attempt every idea, and many will pick out small ideas from within the larger suggested activities. It is also possible to select activities from one occasion to use as part of a completely different event. Each church family is best placed to know what will work in their own locality. Sometimes trial and error will be needed to find out what will work and what will not. The suggestions are for traditional churches and fresh expressions of church alike.

At the same time, the range of talents and experience within the church family will dictate which of the ideas in the book can be most easily and effectively used. For example, if no one has any enthusiasm for organising outdoor sports, then don't do them! On the other hand, a wealth of musical talent may give a strong lead for events and activities involving music. Do not hesitate to draw in outside talent and experience. For smaller churches, in particular, willingness to invite non-church members to contribute their skills or energy can enable a new venture to take place. Being asked to help, whether with technical expertise or making refreshments, can help to draw someone closer into the church family.

Many of the ideas are for families, children and adults, to enjoy together or alongside one another. Where parents are at an early stage on their faith journey, they often appreciate being able to learn at the same level and pace as their children. The adults do not have to admit their ignorance or their inability to follow what more experienced Christians take for granted. This has been amply demonstrated by the Messy Church approach. Experience suggests that many families prefer to attend all-age events when the opportunity arises, as so much time these days is spent on individual pursuits. Equally, there is growing evidence that children are more likely to continue into adult faith when they have good contact with adult Christian role models who take their own faith seriously. However, many of the suggestions included are also suitable to use with children on their own.

The book also includes suggestions for the church to join in community events as 'salt and light', as Christ commanded us.

Isaiah the prophet said:

On this mountain the Lord All-Powerful will prepare for all nations a feast of the finest foods. Choice wines and the best meats will be served. Here the Lord will strip away the burial clothes that cover the nations. The Lord All-Powerful will destroy the power of death and wipe away all tears. No longer will his people be insulted everywhere. The Lord has spoken! At that time, people will say, 'The Lord has saved us! Let's celebrate. We waited and hoped—now our God is here.' (Isaiah 25:6–9)

*

How to use this book

Getting started

This book provides hundreds of ideas, large and small, for churches to try. Pray for the Holy Spirit to guide you as you read through the different sections and see which ideas seem fun or possible in your church. Make a short list of possibilities. Ask two or three other people to read the book and get them to list the ideas that appealed to them. Then compare your lists and see where you are prompted to focus your efforts.

At this stage, look at a calendar. Some of the suggestions may take the best part of a year to plan and produce. An effective 'Out of the church' event (see page 185), for example, could not be staged at short notice and would be a huge undertaking for churches unused to such initiatives. It is far better to select some of the smaller ideas—for example, gathering 'thank you' prayers at harvest time (see page 54), or persuading people to 'donate' their bonus Leap Year day to a good cause (see page 118)—to get something to happen quickly and to gain some experience.

It is important that mission initiatives of the kind proposed in this book are fully supported by the church. At the very least, the parochial church council (PCC), or its equivalent in other denominations, needs to minute that it is content for a particular event or proposal to go ahead, to ensure that it is covered by the church council's insurance policy. Some churches find it easier to set up a Mission and Outreach working party, which reports to the church council, to be responsible for the organisation of mission activities. Clear lines of communication are important. Although in some denominations children and young people may not be members of the church council until their 16th or, in some cases, their 18th birthday, there is no reason why children should not be invited to membership of a Mission Group that reports to a church council.

Putting it into practice

Bible link

Always be joyful and never stop praying. Whatever happens, keep thanking God because of Jesus Christ. This is what God wants you to do.
1 THESSALONIANS 5:16–18

All mission begins with God. He has sent us his good news through his Son, Jesus, and he calls us to share that good news. We are called to join in God's work of mission. So it is not all our responsibility. On the other hand, we are called to provide the events and build the relationships so that God can speak and work through us.

Prayer

Prayer is essential for an idea to flourish. Pray as you look through the ideas in this book and ask God to guide you to appropriate activities for your church to try. Pray as you share your vision with others. Pray as you pause to listen further to the prompting of the Holy Spirit. Pray as you plan and prepare. Pray as the event or activity takes place. Invite people to pray who may not be able to attend: this is a valuable ministry that older or housebound people can undertake. Finally, pray as you clear up, and pray, in thanksgiving, as you review what has taken place.

Purpose

Be clear about what you hope to gain by holding a particular event or campaign. A clearly defined purpose or aim means that you will be able to review whether you achieved it after the event.

Passion

Passion is essential for any idea to come into being. Trying an activity or putting on an event because someone thought it might be a good idea often leads to disappointment. One person with passion can 'parent' an idea to birth. They will need the practical support and the thoughtful discernment of others, but often it will take just one or two people to enthuse a whole team.

Preparation

Preparation is essential for any idea to come into being. The 80:20 rule applies here: expect 80 per cent of the time and effort to go into planning and preparation, and just 20 per cent to the delivery of the actual activity. Find someone who enjoys administration to help with this.

Be realistic about the resources available: people, premises, time and costs.

Preparation checklist

- Pray.
- Choose the occasion and decide how to mark it. Ensure that the church council has adopted the decision.
- Decide the date, if necessary, and book the venue.
- Recruit helpers and start sharing out responsibilities.
- Plan the detail of the event, creating a running order and compiling a kit list. Arrange to borrow any equipment.
- Develop the publicity and consent forms (if required).
- Provide any specific training that is required.
- Start taking bookings (if the event requires them).
- Walk through the event on-site to check the running order and what equipment will be required. Do the risk assessments at the same time. Adjust the kit list or running order if necessary after the on-site visit.

- Pause for prayer to remember the original vision for the event, and listen once more to God.
- Enjoy the event.
- Review how things went and make a note of anything that needs to be altered or improved in future.
- Pray with joy and thanksgiving.

Payment

Putting on an event or activity can be expensive. Try to avoid charging an admission fee to cover the cost of the event if at all possible. It is far better to invite donations to a named charity.

Sources of funding can include donations from individuals who are excited by the mission potential of the event; the mission fund of the church, or of the local diocese or circuit or national denomination; local authority funds; local trust funds; local 'business into the community' initiatives (watch the local newspaper for details); national initiatives to support work with under 5s, young carers, teenagers, older people, social inclusion and so on (these include lottery funding, government schemes and charity projects).

Supermarkets and local businesses will often provide small-scale sponsorship in kind, particularly to help with refreshments. Scrap stores are a good and cheap source of craft and decorative materials. They also sometimes offer surplus production and rejects of commercial stock, such as mugs, plastic beakers or paper cups, and cutlery to use for refreshments, as well as paper, offcuts of plastic and so on. Diocesan (or equivalent) resources centres may have catering, craft or projection equipment for hire. Toy libraries will often have large play equipment for cheap hire. Some local associations of the YMCA also have activity equipment to borrow or hire. Ask around or put a request in the local newspaper to locate what may be available.

Publicity

Publicity is essential to inform the community about the event. Posters and fliers should tell people what they need to know. For example:

- Date
- Time
- Place
- Type of event
- Who is invited
- Where further information can be obtained
- The church or group organising the event

Also register the details on activities websites that do not charge for postings, such as www.wherecanwego.com, to achieve wider publicity. Even if no one attends the event because of the listing, it will at least have indicated to the wider community that there are Christian events taking place.

Personal invitation

Personal invitation works far better—provided that the person doing the inviting is convinced about the quality and value of the event they are publicising. Make the invitation:

- Positive ('it is going to be really good')
- Practical ('yes, there is good access for wheelchairs and buggies')
- Polite (allow people the space to say 'no')
- Proactive ('would you like me to call for you/give you a lift?')

Contact anyone who is already known to the church, particularly couples who were married there and families who have brought their child for baptism or a service of thanksgiving. They have already indicated that they are open to the work of the church, even if at a superficial level.

Invite anyone attending something organised by the church to give their email address to receive invitations to future events. Provide a list on which they can enter their details, including a column for their consent signature. Be tactful. People who find their way to church for one of the memorial occasions, such as All Souls' Day or a time of remembrance for road traffic victims (see page 70), may not wish to be accosted to 'sign up', although the list can be left on show. On other occasions, inviting people to add their email address is a good reason to enter into conversation with them.

Promotion

Promotion fits halfway between publicity and personal invitation. A good example would be arranging with a school to stand at the gate at the end of the day to hand out free Fairtrade chocolate or biscuit bars along with a printed invitation to attend a harvest service or event. The local press could be invited along to take photographs of the promotion, or the organisers could take their own photographs to send to the local paper, accompanied by a press release. Other ideas for promotion include handing out a plain orange with an invitation to a Christingle event; giving out apples with a sticker advertising an alternative Hallowe'en event; giving away pots of bubbles with an invitation to a family event; distributing little packets of seeds to publicise a Good Friday or Easter event. (Seeds, as a symbol of death and new life, are particularly appropriate here, although those receiving them may not be aware of the nuance. Tiny packets can be filled from larger packs to keep down costs.) The school gate is the most obvious place for such a promotion, but other possibilities are:

- Taking a stall in a market or shopping centre to give out Christmas cards that include details of Christmas services, or the Christmas goody bags described on page 87.

- Arranging to visit a toddler group to give the parents and carers a sachet of bubble bath or hand lotion, along with an invite to a 'pamper night'.
- Taking a stall at a village, town or church fête to hand out a free craft item, such as a packet of stickers, or a bag containing instructions and the craft items required to make something, to invite people to a 'crafternoon' or an event that will involve making crafts. It would be effective to hand out Messy Church pencils, along with a flier, to publicise a Messy Church event, not least because these provide the reassurance of a 'brand'.[1]

Plan ahead

Plan to have the next event ready to advertise as people leave the current one. Hand out invitations with early details of what will be happening next. This allows people to put the date in their diary as well as conveying a sense of purpose. It will be necessary to invite them again nearer the next event, but the initial publicity will have been done. This is a little like a shop offering a discount voucher to use on a return visit.

Provide

Provide an attractive bookstall for people to browse during an event or after a service. One church that invited families to a celebration of baptism service and tea displayed a range of 'first' and 'toddler' Bibles as well as some Bible storybooks for parents to buy. Nearly half of the stock was sold, far more than had been anticipated. Christian bookshops are often willing to supply a small range of books on sale-or-return, or to provide sample copies of which more can be ordered. Match the books and cards on sale to the group of people most likely to be attending. When shopping is considered to be the major leisure activity, it makes sense to provide the opportunity to buy something.

Provide good-quality refreshments. When many people are

regular visitors to coffee shops, instant coffee can seem less than welcoming. Avoid having a saucer for donations towards the refreshments; church members can make their own contribution in another way if they wish. Free refreshments are a way to offer welcome and service to visitors and those who only attend occasionally.

Protection of children and vulnerable adults

Protection of those who are vulnerable is essential in any project. Full information on safeguarding can be found through the Independent Safeguarding Authority[2] and the Churches' Child Protection Advisory Service.[3] Churches are advised to consult the Child Protection policy of their own diocese, circuit or denomination to ensure that they comply with its recommendations. The key points to remember are:

- Never be alone with a child or a vulnerable adult.
- Ensure that all activities involving children can be easily observed from outside the meeting room (leave the door open if necessary).
- Have at least two adults to work with any group of children.
- Make sure that adults leaving children in the care of the church complete a consent form that includes a contact telephone number, details of any allergies or medical requirements, a note of specific additional needs of the child, and permission to use photography (if required).

Exercise 'granny care' by aiming to look after any children in the same way you would look after a grandchild. However, if children attend an event in the company of their parents or carers, make sure that the adults know they remain responsible for their own children.

Also provide a first aid kit, an accident or incident book and access to a mobile phone.

Undertake a 'risk assessment' of any activity to identify any potential hazards and plan to reduce the risk of accidents. A full range of advice on ensuring the safety of children and young people can be found on the 'Barnabas in churches' website.[4]

Photography

To comply with the Data Protection Act 1998, permission must be granted by the parent or carer before any images of a child can be taken. Include a question about permission to photograph children on any consent form used. If parents do not give their permission, it is essential that the child is given a sticky coloured label to wear, to indicate to photographers that they should avoid getting that particular child in shot.

At events where consent forms are not required, where children remain the responsibility of their parents, it is still good practice to have clear notices explaining that photographs may be taken and that families can opt out by wearing one of the coloured labels.

It is well worth requesting permission to photograph children, as photos are an important way of publicising what the church is doing. Adults, of course, can answer for themselves.

Photographs can be used to:

- Create a display in the church to show the sort of events that take place.
- Send to the local press to accompany a report of an event.
- Include in publicity about future events.
- Build an archive of recent church history (useful for a 'do you remember?' event, or to review the year).

Seasonal activities

*

— An activity for autumn —

St Michael and All Angels (Michaelmas)

Date: 29 September

Web link

www.angelfestival.org.uk

Introduction

Research, by Steve Hollinghurst among others, suggests that there is increasing interest in angels in 21st-century Britain. This means that an angel event will be attractive. The outline is focused on the feast of Michael and All Angels, but it could be easily adapted to run in Advent or over Christmas. This could be an event particularly for younger children. On the other hand, the accounts of the archangels Gabriel, Michael and Raphael do have a harder edge for boys; this makes it a possible event for primary-aged children or all ages together.

Key Bible verses

God will command his angels to protect you wherever you go.
PSALM 91:11

All you mighty angels, who obey God's commands, come and praise your Lord!
PSALM 103:20

Bible links

- 1 Kings 19:1–8 (Elijah is comforted by an angel)
- Daniel 3 (Daniel's three friends are rescued by an angel)
- Acts 12:1–11 (Peter is released by an angel)
- Matthew 18:10 (Jesus tells us that we have a guardian angel to look after us)
- Revelation 12:7–12 (Archangel Michael and his angels attack the dragon)

Key focus

Sharing the Christian story; fundraising for charity (by charging for admission in aid of a named charity)

Key group

Church family; schools; local community

Activity ideas

Preparation

Send out angel-shaped invitations. Invite people to wear angel fancy dress (or create some angel costumes as part of the activities). Make a large display of the memory verse chosen for the session, using either Psalm 91:11 or Psalm 103:20. You may wish to consider decorating the meeting space or changing the lighting to be in pastel shades.

Ask at the beginning what the children already know about angels. They are most likely to mention the nativity and Easter morning angels. Smaller children may be confused between angels and fairies, so be ready to explain that angels are God's messengers who look after us, but they do not do magic or grant wishes.

Story

Tell the story of Daniel in the lions' den. This emphasises the triumph of good over evil. Read it from a children's Bible or storybook if no one is willing to perform it. Talk about what are the 'lions' that we are afraid of and who the angels are that God sends to help us. Explain that Jesus told us that we have guardian angels in heaven to look after us (Matthew 18:10) and use the story of the lost sheep that follows on in Matthew's Gospel, to explain how God looks after us.

Songs

- God's people aren't super-brave, super-heroes (see song list on page 207)
- My God is so big, so strong and so mighty (see song list on page 208).

Four activity areas

If you have a small group, everyone can move around the activities together. With a bigger group, divide everyone into four smaller groups to visit each activity in turn, so that no area is too busy.

Area 1: Elijah being comforted by the angel

You will need a children's Bible or storybook version of 1 Kings 19:1–8; small paper plates; small card discs; glue sticks; scissors; colouring pens; glitter (optional).

Tell the story and then talk about times when we are scared or tired, and explain that God is always with us.

Make a paper plate angel by cutting the plate in half, across the diameter. The flat edge of one half of the circle becomes the bottom of the angel. Cut the other piece in half again to make two quarters.

Stick the two quarters at the back of the angel's body to become wings. Add the card disc to be the head and decorate with pens and glitter (optional). Note: the angel lies flat, rather than standing up.[1]

Area 2: Shadrach, Meshach and Abednego are looked after by an angel in the fiery furnace

You will need a children's Bible or storybook version of Daniel 3:1–30; a red scarf and a white scarf (or lengths of material); enough space to run around.

Tell the story and then play a version of 'tag', with one person being fire (identified by having the red scarf tied to their wrist) to catch people. When people have been 'tagged' by fire, they have to stand still. A second person acts as the angel (identified by the white scarf) who can release them. Make sure everyone who wants to be either fire or an angel has a turn.

Area 3: Peter is released from chains by an angel

You will need a children's Bible or storybook version of Acts 12:1–11; a supply of paper chain links;[2] pens.

Tell the story and then talk about the chains that stop us from doing the good things that Jesus wants us to do. Create a long chain. (Older children may want to write down some of the 'chains' they have just discussed on to individual links of paper chains.) Then act out the story of Peter being released, with one person taking the part of Peter, who is wrapped in the paper chains that have been made. Someone else arrives as the angel, tells Peter to get up and helps pull off all the chains.

Area 4: Everyone has a guardian angel

You will need the chosen memory verse displayed on an A3 sheet of paper (either Psalm 91:11 or Matthew 18:10), laid flat on a table or the floor; three saucers of different coloured paint; paper towel or wet wipes to wipe thumbs clean; felt pens; glitter (optional).

Explain that Jesus told us that everyone has a guardian angel, a special angel who looks after us. Ask everyone to dip their thumb into paint and then make a thumb-print on to the memory verse display. Do this first so that the paint can dry a little.

Learn the chosen memory verse by chanting it together several times. Then divide the group into two and ask each half to say alternate words. Swap over so that the groups say the words they missed out last time. Finally chant it together again. Now everyone can add drawn wings and other features (and glitter, if used) to turn their thumbprint into a mini-portrait of their own guardian angel. Make sure all hands are clean before moving to the next activity.

Refreshments

Try to provide 'white' or 'angel' food for refreshments, such as vanilla ice cream; lemonade and milk; mini meringues; rice cakes; white bread sandwiches; butterfly cakes as 'angel cakes'; angel-shaped biscuits.

Teaching and sending out

Explain that all the angels we have heard about today were messengers in the Bible, bringing news from God. God also wants us to be messengers for him, to share with other people the good news about Jesus' love. Light a candle and invite everyone to think for a few moments of someone whom they could tell about Jesus and how much he loves them.

— Prayer —

May the Lord send his angel to guide us on our way and keep us safe.

Developing the theme

Michaelmas is an ideal time to take the opportunity to run an 'angels and dragons' party. Invite everyone to come in fancy dress, dressed as an angel or dragon. The venue could be decked with white balloons and red and orange streamers. Themed games could include sleeping dragons (like sleeping lions); pin the tail on the dragon; musical angels (statues); dragon quest (hunt the thimble) and 'pass the angel' (getting into teams, standing in a line and passing a white balloon down the line without using hands). Party food could include decorating cupcakes to create angel-wing cakes (like butterfly cakes). Help the children to slice off a thin top layer of the cake, spread some buttercream icing or soft cheese on to the cake, and use the sliced-off layer to create two wings, which need to be gently inserted into the icing. To drink, you could make 'dragon's breath drinks' by adding a scoop of ice cream to a fizzy drink.

Developing the theme on a grand scale

To build on the evident interest in angels, challenge the whole community to stage an angel festival. Many rural communities hold scarecrow festivals where families, schools and businesses make a scarecrow to display over a weekend. Holy Trinity Church, Ripon, developed the idea to focus on angels. Read their inspiring story, see the pictures and get ideas from www.angelfestival.org.uk. The success of this Hope 08 project demonstrates that the idea works well in an urban context.

These ideas could be easily adapted to run during Advent or over the Christmas period. A 'Christmas angel' breakfast or tea could quickly become a new tradition.

*

— An activity for winter —

Interactive crib experience

Date: from Advent Sunday for seven weeks, through to the week after Epiphany

Web link

www.getinthepicture.org.uk

Introduction

The aim of this activity is to encourage people to visit a crib scene several times during the changing seasons of Advent, Christmas and Epiphany, to take part in different reflective activities on each occasion. The most obvious place to do this is in church, where the church's own crib set will provide the focus for the activities. However, it is also possible to set it up in a school, perhaps in the entrance area, or in a local library or children's centre. Churches working closely with a children's hospice could offer this activity for children, families and staff to share.

The publicity should make it clear when the crib can be visited, as well as the dates when each phase of activities will start. Provide a hard-backed 'visitors' book for people to note down their experience of going to see the crib, or to make prayer requests, as well as lots of paper and colouring things.

Ensure that there is a welcoming sign outside with a clear invitation to take part, and make sure that the door is open if at all possible. (A closed door beside a suggestion to enter does not always look enticing.) If this is a new activity in the area, make sure that the local media know what is going to take place. If they cannot send a photographer, invite a family to try out some of the activities, to be photographed and to give some quotes that you can send to the local newspaper.

If possible, provide tealight candles for people to light in response to their experience. This may mean that the interactive crib can only be available when the church is supervised. For example, some churches may advertise that they will be open for the interactive crib experience between, say, 3pm and 5pm, Saturdays–Mondays, to ensure that everything can be supervised and that there are people available to chat and support.

The aim is to encourage visitors to 'step into' the part of the different characters as the crib scene is updated each week. Providing different dressing-up clothes for each phase will help children to do this. There are also instructions for adults and children to help them to imagine being part of the story. Make sure that the Key Bible verse(s) for each phase of the journey is clearly displayed. Finally, there is a different prayer for each stage of the journey.

The directions below suggest changing the focus and activities each week for seven weeks, from the beginning of Advent through to Epiphany. However, it is also possible to offer the material for weeks one and two together for most of Advent; weeks three to six together, to be available from the Sunday before Christmas until the New Year; and week seven in early January. Each week, write the Bible verse, instructions and prayer out on pieces of card and display them near the crib scene so that people can reflect at their own pace.

Key Bible verses

- Luke 1:38 (Mary obeys Gabriel's message)
- Luke 2:4–5 (Joseph and Mary travel to Bethlehem)
- Luke 2:7 (Mary's baby is born)
- Luke 2:13–14 (Angels praise God)
- Luke 2:15–20 (Shepherds visit Mary's baby)
- Matthew 2:9–10 (The star shows the way)
- Matthew 2:1–2 (Wise men look for a baby)

Key focus

Sharing the Christian story; providing sacred space for reflection

Key group

Church family, schools, local community, families

Activity ideas

Week One: Surprise and obedience

You will need the Bible verse displayed in full (Luke 1:38); the crib scene set up with Mary and Gabriel and nothing else visible; party poppers for children to release or pots of bubbles to play with; dressing-up clothes (angel wings, and a blue robe with a white headdress).

Display several different reproductions of paintings of the annunciation. These can be displayed on PowerPoint or printed out.[3]

Instructions

This week's theme is surprise and obedience. What is surprising in your life at the moment? In what ways are you being obedient to God? In what ways might you be avoiding God's call?

Instructions for children

If you would like to, you may dress up as Mary or the angel, Gabriel. Mary was very surprised by the visit from Gabriel. Pop a party popper or blow some bubbles as you think about Mary being surprised.

— Prayer —

God of surprises, help us to obey your amazing commands.

Week Two: Travelling

You will need the Bible verses displayed in full (Luke 2:4–5); dressing-up clothes (blue robe with a white headdress, a brown robe and a wooden staff, simple sandals).

Changing the crib

Change the crib scene to show Joseph and Mary; remove the angel Gabriel, the images of the annunciation, and the previous week's activities.

Instructions

This week's theme is 'travelling'. Reflect on where you will be travelling this Christmas. Who will you meet? What will the journey be like?

Instructions for children

Walk slowly around the church and imagine that you are travelling towards Bethlehem, like Mary and Joseph. Imagine not knowing where you are going to sleep tonight.

— Prayer —

Faithful God, thank you that you have promised to be with us wherever we go.

Week Three: Being

You will need the Bible verse displayed in full (Luke 2:7); dressing-up clothes (baby shawl or blanket); a single lit candle (for reasons of safety, this could be an electric or battery-powered one).[4]

Changing the crib

Place the baby in the manger. Remove Joseph and Mary and the previous week's activities.

Instructions

This week's theme is about 'being'. Babies cannot do anything apart from 'be' and yet they are treasured. Who has God made you to be?

Instructions for children

Sit quietly, looking at the candle, and think about how small you used to be, and how much you have changed and grown. What can you do now that you could not do two years ago?

— Prayer —

God of love, thank you for loving us just as we are.

Week Four: Sharing God's good news

You will need the Bible verses displayed in full (Luke 2:13–14); dressing-up clothes (angel wings and a white robe).

Changing the crib

Leave baby Jesus and add the angel(s) to the crib. Remove the previous week's activities.

Instructions

This week's theme is about sharing God's good news, just as the angels brought good news to the shepherds. How will the good news be heard in the world this year? What hinders God's good news from being heard? How can you help God's message to be heard?

Instructions for children

Sit quietly and listen to the sounds you hear: sounds outside, sounds in the church and sounds in yourself, like your heartbeat or breathing. Ask God to put a special thought into your mind as you sit quietly.

— Prayer —

God of hope, help us to share your good news.

Week Five: Surprise and joy

You will need the Bible verses displayed in full (Luke 2:15–20); dressing-up clothes (dark robes for shepherds, and teatowel head-dresses); supply of drawing materials (paper or thin card, colourful pens and pencils and optional glue sticks and glitter).

Changing the crib

Add the shepherds to the crib scene alongside Jesus and the angel(s). Remove the previous week's activities.

Instructions

This week's theme is about surprise and joy. What is surprising in your life at the moment? What is bringing you joy? What do you do with your experiences of joy?

Instructions for children

Draw a picture of surprise and joy. You may need to use lots of bright colours.

— Prayer —

God of joy, help us to be surprised again that you sent your Son to be born as a human baby.

Week Six: Brightness and light

You will need the Bible verses displayed in full (Matthew 2:9–10); dressing-up clothes (headbands with star shapes attached); supply of thin card or thick paper; scissors; glue sticks or sticky tape; instructions for making a Chinese lantern.[5]

Changing the crib

Remove the shepherds and display a star above the crib (make or buy a star if the crib set does not include one). Remove the previous week's activities.

Instructions

This week's theme is about brightness and light. Where do you need the light of the star to shine in your own life, and out in the world? Where do you bring God's light into dark places?

Instructions for children

Make a Chinese lantern, either to take home to remind you of God's light in the world, or to leave in the church to encourage other visitors.

— Prayer —

God of light, may your gifts of love and hope shine
in the dark places of the world.

Week Seven: Studying and learning

You will need the Bible verses displayed in full (Matthew 2:1–2); dressing-up clothes (crowns, headdresses, royal cloaks); supply of ready-cut crown templates; sticky tape; colourful pens; adhesive play-jewels;[6] optional glue sticks and glitter.

Changing the crib

Add the wise men alongside Jesus and the star. Remove the previous week's activities.

Instructions

This week's theme is about studying and learning. What are you learning at the moment? How can that learning be offered back to God? In what ways could you put the same effort into finding God as the wise men did?

Instructions for children

Make a paper crown, or decorate a ready-cut template, to wear to go home.

— Prayer —

God of wisdom, inspire us to learn more about you and your ways.

Developing the theme

Some churches may wish to start this project in a small way the first year. Offer a 'get into the picture' opportunity for children or whole families to dress up in nativity clothes provided by the church, with an appropriate backdrop, to have their photograph taken. Either offer the services of a photographer, with a single copy printed out immediately and the opportunity to buy more copies, or invite families to take their own pictures. Visit www.getinthepicture.org.uk for further ideas.

*

— An activity for spring —

Good Friday gathering (or 'Walk through Easter')

Date: Good Friday or during Holy Week

Web links

www.experienceeaster.org
www.easterjourney.org.uk

Introduction

As many people are not at school or work on Good Friday, this is a good day to share the account of the events of Holy Week and Easter. Some people will mark Easter by attending an event on Good Friday, in the same way that they will mark Christmas by attending a carol service.

Key Bible verse

'God bless the one who comes in the name of the Lord.'
MATTHEW 21:9

Bible links

Jesus' entry into Jerusalem, and the Last Supper, passion, crucifixion and resurrection narratives from the Gospels:

- Matthew 21:1–17; 26:17—28:9
- Mark 11:1–11; 14:22—16:8
- Luke 19:28–40; 22:7—24:12
- John 12:12–17; 13:1–10; 18:1—20:10

Key focus

Sharing the Christian story; providing sacred space for reflection

Key group

Church family; school; local community; families

Activity ideas

You will need one person to act the part of Jesus, rehearsed in advance (this could be an older teenager, and it would be helpful if they have a cloak to wear so they can be easily identified in the midst of all the activities); a narrator with a copy of the script, rehearsed in advance; paper, scissors and sticky tape to make palm branches;[7] pre-mixed bread dough; greaseproof paper; clingfilm; antibacterial wipes or gel; washed apples and bananas; table knives; drinks; spread or jam to put on bread rolls; small pre-cut card or wooden crosses about 8cm long;[8] an Easter garden display; the story *Where is Jesus?* by Margery Francis[9] or the account of Easter morning in a children's Bible; the songs 'Give me oil in my lamp', 'Lord of the Dance' or 'There is singing in the desert' (see page 207).

Gathering

While everyone is assembling, invite them to make a palm branch to wave.

Presentation

Narrator: Today we are going to follow Jesus in the last week of his life on earth. We will be with him as he rides into Jerusalem on a donkey. We will imagine being in the room when he ate a special meal with his disciples. We will pray with him in the garden of Gethsemane, and we will find out what happened at the end of that week.

(Prayer) We pray that God will send his Holy Spirit to inspire all the activities of this gathering so that we may learn more about the events of Holy Week and Easter.

Narrator: Hooray for the Son of David! God bless the one who comes in the name of the Lord. Hooray for God in heaven above!

The narrator teaches actions to the verse (Matthew 21:9) as follows.

Narrator / All: Hooray for the Son of David!
(Everyone crouches down and jumps up)

Narrator / All: God bless the one who comes...
(Everyone points up to heaven)

Narrator / All: ... in the name of the Lord.
(Everyone points across the room and then turns around)

Narrator / All: Hooray for God...
(Everyone crouches down and jumps up)

Narrator / All: ... in heaven above!
(Everyone points up to heaven)

Narrator: As Jesus came to Jerusalem *(enter 'Jesus')* with his disciples, he got on to a donkey to ride into the city. *('Jesus' walks round the room)* The disciples and the crowd began to wave branches taken from palm trees (everyone waves their branch) and they began to shout, 'Hooray for the Son of David...' *(Everyone shouts the memory verse twice)*

Song: 'Give me oil in my lamp'. Use the palm branches to wave as everyone processes round the meeting space while the song is being sung.

Narrator: Jesus and his friends went to Jerusalem to celebrate the Passover festival together. They ate the special Passover meal. We are going to share that meal later, but now we are going to prepare the food so it will be ready for us.

Preparing the feast

Provide everyone with a small ball of pre-mixed dough to knead and form into a small roll. The dough can be sweetened with sugar if you wish. When ready, the rolls should be laid on to squares of greaseproof paper. Write the person's name on the greaseproof paper. Start baking immediately in a pre-heated oven. Older children and adults can also help to cut up washed fruit into segments. The segments can be stored in bowls covered with clingfilm. NB: provide antibacterial wipes for hands and work surfaces before handling food. Involve everyone in clearing up from the roll-making before moving on to the next activity.

Narrator: Jesus went into the temple in Jerusalem. It was a huge building where people went to worship God. But it was also like a tourist attraction where visitors needed to change their money into a different currency or to buy doves to sacrifice as part of their worship. Jesus was shocked at the way people were misusing God's house. He began to send all the traders out of the temple.

Game

Invite everyone to find a space where they can act as if they are selling things. Talk about what things might have been on sale (such as pigeons for sacrifices, food and so on) and then ask everyone to make as much noise as possible. When the person playing Jesus enters the noisy market place, he stands in the centre of the room with his head bowed. When he starts to whirl around, everyone must freeze and be quiet. If the person playing Jesus notices anyone moving, he points at them and they have to sit down at the side of the room. Continue until everyone has been eliminated, or until the game has lost its fun.

Refreshments

If possible, sit at long tables to share the Passover meal. These can be set up during the previous games and drama. The person playing Jesus sits at one of the tables to eat the bread which has now been baked, the fruit and cups of water or fruit juice. Provide spread or jam to serve with the bread, or add sugar to the original mix to make it sweet.

Narrator: After Jesus and his friends had finished eating this special meal, they went out of Jerusalem to find a quiet place to pray. Jesus spent most of the night praying to God, because he knew he was going to be killed on the cross the next day. I am going to say a prayer now, as we think about being quiet together with Jesus.

(Prayer) Lord Jesus, the disciples fell asleep while you were praying that night. Help us to be quiet with you for a few moments now.

Drama

Prepare a few people to act as soldiers who will burst into the activity to arrest Jesus and march him away, out of sight. These could be adults or older children. Before the soldiers enter, play a game of 'sleeping disciples' by inviting everyone to lie still and quiet on the floor until the soldiers burst in. The soldiers take Jesus away.

Craft

Explain that Jesus was taken away to be killed on a cross. Provide a small pre-cut card or wooden cross, about 8cm long, for each person. Invite everyone to write or draw on their cross as they think about Jesus being killed.

Easter garden

Move to look at an Easter garden that has already been created. Discuss what can be seen: the three crosses, the stone across the entrance to the tomb, and the flowers.

Story

Read *Where is Jesus?* by Margery Francis or the account of Easter morning in a children's Bible, to help the youngest children to understand that the crucifixion is not the end of the story.

Reappearance

As the story ends, the person playing Jesus appears again in the distance. Point this out to everyone.

Song: 'Lord of the Dance' or 'There is singing in the desert'

Narrator: *(Prayer)* Father God, today we are sad to remember that Jesus was killed on the cross that first Good Friday. Help us to be joyful on Sunday when we celebrate that he came back to life in a new way.

Developing the theme

This event could be run in a school to help pupils and staff experience the Easter story, or in church for primary-age pupils to visit during Holy Week. Further ideas to develop this theme can be found on the websites above (see page 36).

*

— An activity for summer —

St James' Day

Date: 25 July

Web links

www.labyrinth.org.uk
www.lostinwonder.org.uk
www.barnabasinchurches.org.uk/8065 (to download sample prayer stations sheet)

Introduction

St James is the patron saint of pilgrims, so this is a good time of year to offer a pilgrimage experience, although it could take place at other times of the year.

Key Bible verse

I will lead the blind on roads they have never known; I will guide them on paths they have never travelled. Their road is dark and rough, but I will give light to keep them from stumbling. This is my solemn promise.

ISAIAH 42:16

Bible links

- Matthew 4:18–22 (James accepts Jesus' invitation to follow him)
- Matthew 17:1–3 (Jesus takes James, with Peter and John, up a high mountain)
- Acts 2:28 (Jesus shows us the path of life)

Key focus

Sharing the Christian story; providing sacred space for reflection

Key group

Church family; local community; families

Activity ideas

This activity will work best with pilgrims of all ages travelling together to enjoy each other's company and insights. Before setting off, share a Bible reading for the beginning of the pilgrimage, such as Matthew 4:18–22, which recounts the call of the first disciples, including James. Call forward each person taking part in the pilgrimage, ask them to announce their name and give them a sticker to wear with a shell shape drawn on it. Finally, pray the following prayer.

— Prayer —

Father God, you call us by name to follow you just as you called St James. Guide our journey today so that we may learn more of your great love for us. We pray for safety for everyone who travels in your name. Amen

Plan a circular route around the locality to visit significant places in the community to pray, such as schools, pubs, playgrounds and shops. In each of these places, focus prayers on learning, food for the journey, places for refreshment or people who serve us, as appropriate. It might be possible to set up prayer encounters in advance at the places where you intend to stop. Otherwise, use the same set of simple responses, adapted for each place. For example:

Leader: The Lord is here.
Response: His Spirit is with us.
Leader: We pray for God's blessing on this (school). May all who work here know welcome, safety and peace. Lord, in your mercy...
Response: Hear our prayer.

Groups may also wish to learn a Bible verse, such as Acts 2:28, to say aloud at each stopping place along the route. Have one person to lead the group and to be responsible for leading prayer at each stop, and another person, who is also familiar with the planned route, to walk behind the group to make sure no one gets lost. Arrange for someone to carry a first aid kit and a mobile phone for possible emergencies.

Use Matthew 17:1–3 at the end of the pilgrimage to show that James was taken to amazing places and had amazing experiences because he was willing to leave where he was to follow Jesus. Provide everyone with a traditional scallop shell to take home as a reminder of their pilgrimage (even if it is just cut out of card).

— Prayer —

Heavenly Father, give us the courage, just like St James, to get up and follow you wherever you call us to serve you. We have no idea where our Christian journey will take us, so help us to trust you.

Developing the theme

In areas that are less safe to walk around, or for a variation, another idea would be to organise different prayer stations inside the church or hall, which everyone has to visit to complete their pilgrimage, before ending with a shared meal. These prayer stations could be based on the main features of the church building, such as a pillar, the font, altar, pulpit, lectern, a window and so on.

You might wish to use short reflections, such as the example below. Further examples can be found on the Barnabas website: www.barnabasinchurches.org.uk/8065.

Pillar

Our church is a big solid building. The pillars help to hold up the roof. Feel how hard the pillar is. Look up at the roof high above.

Dear God, thank you that we have safe houses to live in.

Jesus said, 'Anyone who hears and obeys these teachings of mine and obeys them is like a wise person who built a house on solid rock' (Matthew 7:24).

Another possibility is to set up a labyrinth for people to journey around. This can also be provided as an online experience. Find out more about labyrinths at www.labyrinth.org.uk or explore the online version from the Methodist Church at www.lostinwonder.org.uk.

Of course, this idea can be used on any occasion, not just linked to St James' day.

Mission ideas for Autumn (September, October and November)

Since the 13th century, September has been linked with people going away to university and school to start a new season of study. In times past, they often would not return until the following early summer, when the roads improved and more help was needed on the land. These days, the autumn still feels a good time to start new things. Certainly the start of a new school year and the move away from the long, light evenings of summer seem to prompt many people to try a new activity or learn a new skill. For some churches, autumn is a good time to focus afresh on mission. It is interesting that 'Back to Church' Sunday has been timed for the last Sunday in September, as it seems to tie in with this season of new beginnings.

September and October offer mission opportunities linked with harvest and the environment. Then, as autumn progresses, both the church and the national calendars move into a period of remembering, with All Saints and All Souls Days, as well as Bonfire Night and Remembrance.

*

Holy Cross Day

Date: 14 September

Web link

www.barnabasinchurches.org.uk (search for *A-cross the World*)

Introduction

Traditionally, Holy Cross Day celebrates the finding of the True Cross in Jerusalem in AD325 by St Helena, mother of the Roman Emperor Constantine. Christians, particularly in the Eastern traditions, commemorate the cross, which was the means by which Jesus brought about God's plan of salvation.

Key Bible verse

The message about the cross doesn't make any sense to lost people. But for those of us who are being saved, it is God's power at work.

1 CORINTHIANS 1:18

Bible links

- Matthew 16:24; Mark 8:34 (taking up the cross and following Jesus' life of service)
- John 19:16–30 (Jesus is nailed to a cross)
- Hebrews 12:2 (fixing our eyes on Jesus, who did not give up because of the cross)

Key focus

Sharing the Christian story

Key group

Church family; schools

Activity ideas

Provide a supply of small crosses, wooden or card, arranged around the base of a large cross. Explain that it is not always easy to live as Jesus wants us to live: to be generous and kind, to put the needs of other people before our own, and to work to put right the wrongs in the world. Jesus instructed his disciples to pick up their cross to follow him, forgetting about their own concerns. That is what every Christian is called to do. Invite everyone to reflect quietly on what they feel God is calling them to do at the moment in their home, at school or work, in the community or out in the wider world. When they are ready, ask them to pick up one of the small crosses as they ask God for the strength to carry out the task before them. Play some quiet music during the time of reflection, such as the Taizé chant 'Stay with me'.

Offer everyone in the congregation, or children's group, a small plain wooden cross or one cut from thin card.[1] These can be decorated with felt-tipped pens or crayons. Invite everyone to write or draw something as they respond to thinking about Jesus dying on the cross. If desired, print an appropriate Bible verse on to a small sticky label to apply to the reverse of each cross.

A good book for developing activities based around the cross is *A-cross the World* by Martyn Payne and Betty Pedley. This contains details of the very many diverse styles of cross that are traditional in different countries and cultures, with ideas for making and learning from them.[2]

Prayer

Give everyone a sheet of paper or card with a cross outline. As they pray, invite them to write at the top of the outline the names of people who are leaders in the church family. At the foot, they can write the names of people who have helped their own faith to grow. On one arm, ask them to write the names of people who love and look after them and, on the other arm, the names of people whose faith they can encourage. Finally, in the middle, they can write the names of people who need prayers. Everyone could be invited to hold their cross as they sing a hymn such as 'Lift high the cross', 'Thank you for the cross' or 'When I survey the wondrous cross'.

Developing the theme

Invite people to see how many examples of the cross they can notice during the coming week. The church and churchyard are obvious places to look, but crosses can also be spotted in architecture, on logos, coins and crests, and in secular designs. Older children and teenagers might like to take digital photos of crosses that they find in unusual places to create a PowerPoint display or a photo-montage for the church noticeboard. Discuss why the cross is used so frequently, and whether its use was more common in the past than today.

* * *

Television tie-in

Date: through the autumn

Web links

www.idta.co.uk (International Dance Teachers Association)
www.bita-uk.com (British Ice Teachers Association)

Introduction

These days, a wide range of talent and reality television series have become extremely popular. They often encourage people to try a new skill or experience, or to demonstrate that they are just as talented as the people on television. Churches can arrange to provide an opportunity for all ages to learn or practise a newly popular activity. It is often a good idea to link an activity with a current well-known programme as people will readily understand the nature of the occasion.

Key Bible verse

Very old people with walking sticks will once again sit around in Jerusalem, while boys and girls play in the streets.

ZECHARIAH 8:4–5

Bible links

- Jeremiah 31:4 (we are so precious to God that he will rebuild society so that we can play and dance)
- Matthew 22:10 (go into the streets to invite people to come in)
- Mark 12:31 (love other people)

Key focus

Building community relationships; fundraising for charity; fun

Key group

Children; local community; families

Activity ideas

The television programme *Strictly Come Dancing* has made ballroom and Latin American dancing popular once more. Advertise a ballroom dance event and highlight the fact that expert tuition will be provided. Book a qualified dance instructor (if no one in the church family has the necessary skill) and ask them to lead the majority of the session in 'line-dance' style so that partners are not required.[3] Provide refreshments and make sure that some of the programme's catchphrases are used during the event.

Other popular television programmes include *Dancing on Ice*, which suggests arranging a group visit to an ice rink, and *Last Choir Standing* (which only appeared for one series), which could prompt a session to try barber shop-style singing. Survival skills or eating wild food are also made to look fun on television. Organise an event led by a qualified expert so that people can try surviving in a hostile environment.

The *Dragons' Den* theme could be developed as a way for small groups of people to pitch for a grant of, say, £100, to raise money for a charity. Invite local people to be an audience—they could vote to decide the winning entry. It might be possible to persuade a local business to provide the seed corn prize money.

The team challenge aspect of *The Apprentice* would provide a theme for a group of people to work together to tackle a project in the community. The project could be something simple that would only take a day, such as tidying a garden for a lone-parent family or someone elderly or with physical disabilities, or something larger that will require the group to work together for several weeks, such as renovating some community space or providing a drop-in facility for Sunday afternoons in Advent or Lent. An Apprentice-type group might decide to volunteer to spend time together on an overseas project under the auspices of an aid agency.

— Prayer —

Creator God, thank you for the gift of enjoyment. Help us to enjoy fun activities together as we get to know each other. Amen

Developing the theme

A regular 'tea dance' would be the obvious way to follow up a learn-to-dance event. Ideally, find someone who can dance with reasonable competence to lead the dancing, and someone else to host the event. Organise a proper interval with hot drinks and cakes. Building relationships in this way provides a group of people to invite to 'Back to Church' Sunday or other services particularly suited to guests, if they do not already attend church.

* * *

Harvest

Date: early autumn

Web links

www.christianaid.org.uk
www.ecocongregation.org.uk
www.generous.org.uk (for the 'LOAF' campaign)
www.tearfund.org
www.barnabasinchurches.org.uk/8065 (to download sample activity sheet)

Introduction

Resources to be used at harvest-tide in church, school or the community are produced by many aid agencies. The best often come from Tearfund or Christian Aid, and include many ideas for assemblies and all-age services. An activity session could also be organised with these resources. This might also be the right time to start using some of the Ecocongregation materials (see web link) to encourage church members or the local community to live in accordance with sustainable principles.

Key Bible verses

Be thankful and praise the Lord as you enter his temple. The Lord is good! His love and faithfulness will last for ever.
PSALM 100:4–5

Bible links

- Genesis 8:22 (God promises a harvest)
- Psalm 126 (celebrates the harvest)
- Matthew 15:36 (Jesus always gave thanks before eating)

Key focus

Campaigning and social action; fundraising for charity

Key group

Church family; schools; local community

Activity ideas

As part of offering a traditional service, put a leaflet advertising the Harvest Thanksgiving through every letterbox in the area. Add a tear-off slip asking for suggestions of things for which people would like to give thanks. Provide posting boxes for the responses in a shop, a pub and the school, as well as in the church. The request could also be put in the church, village or area magazine, or even publicised through the local paper by contacting the news desk with a story headed 'Local church wants to say "thanks"'. Develop this idea by escorting older children to knock on doors to ask for ideas to include in the thanksgiving service. Make sure all suggestions are included, even if some editing is required. Invite children in the local school or uniformed organisations to write or draw what they would like to say 'thank you' for. In a very small village with no school, contact children with a personalised letter to ask for contributions.

Ask children to help decorate the church for harvest. They may choose to include items such as model tractors or their own paintings and drawings. Other children may wish to try traditional flower arranging. Advertise and organise simple sports or games in the church or churchyard before the harvest service and serve refreshments (some people will stay for the service itself).

A harvest meal at lunchtime or early evening (bring-and-share in the hall or church, or negotiate a flat-price menu at a pub or café) is a good gathering point. Include the briefest of humorous talks or a slightly extended grace to share something of the gospel. Provide activity sheets with a harvest theme for children (download from the Barnabas website), as well as pens.

Prayer

Create a visual prayer, based on Psalm 126, on a large sheet of paper. On the top third, draw huge clouds in which people can write the things they want to give thanks for, 'celebrated with laughter and joyful songs' (v. 2). On one side at the bottom of the sheet, craft a sand-coloured desert space with a stream running through it and invite people to write their own names as they pray to be 'like streams in the Southern Desert' (v. 4). On the other side, provide a green-coloured space to represent a field where people can write or draw their intercessions (v. 5).

Developing the theme

Another suggestion would be to encourage people to follow the 'LOAF' principle by checking whether the things they buy are either locally produced, organic, farmed in an animal-friendly way or fairly traded.

* * *

St Francis

Date: 4 October

Introduction

St Francis is the patron saint of animals, birds and the environment, so this festival provides an opportunity to celebrate the diversity of creation and our dependence upon it. As Hildegard of Bingen said, 'All creation is a song of praise to God'. St Francis is also thought to have developed the first nativity scene including animals as well as the people we read about in the Gospel accounts.

Key Bible verse

Let all things praise the name of the Lord, because they were created at his command.

PSALM 148:5

Bible links

- Genesis 1:1 (God created everything at the beginning)
- Genesis 1:28 (God puts humans in charge of the earth and all living things)
- Psalm 148 (all of creation is invited to praise God)
- Luke 12:24 (God looks after his creation)

Key focus

Sharing the Christian story; providing sacred space for reflection

Key group

Church family; local community

Activity ideas

Create a visual display to illustrate all of creation being invited to praise God, as outlined in Psalm 148.

In advance, give everyone a copy of Psalm 148 to take home. Alternatively, give everyone a single verse of the psalm to ensure that all verses are covered by at least one person. Ask people to bring an item to church to illustrate something mentioned in the psalm. (If the group is small, ask them to bring two items relating to different verses.) Either down the aisle or around the meeting space, put signs indicating where each verse is to be positioned. The verses should run in sequence. As people arrive, ask them to add their item to the appropriate verse. When all the contributions have been received, work in groups to create a display for each verse. Discuss why people have brought what they have.

After all 14 displays (one for each verse) are complete, invite everyone to wander around to view them. Finally, read Psalm 148 slowly so that everyone can gather near each display in turn for the appropriate verse. Sing 'O, praise ye the Lord', 'All creatures of our God and king' or 'From the ends of the earth', all of which are based on Psalm 148.

Prayer

Help everyone to learn the following prayer, which is attributed to St Francis, by singing it several times.

Make me a channel of your peace.
Where there is hatred, let me bring your love;
Where there is injury, your pardon, Lord;
And where there is doubt, true faith in you.

Oh Master, grant that I may never seek
So much to be consoled as to console,
To be understood as to understand,
To be loved as to love with all my soul.

Make me a channel of your peace.
Where there's despair in life, let me bring hope;
Where there is darkness, only light,
And where there's sadness, ever joy.

For it is in pardoning that we are pardoned,
In giving of ourselves, that we receive
and in dying that we're born
to eternal life. Amen

Developing the theme

Francis-tide is a good time to hold a service of blessing for pets and other animals, perhaps based upon the praise of Psalm 148. This could be held in church if mostly smaller animals are expected. A field is needed for larger and farm animals. This outdoor worship could be the start of a new tradition.

St Francis is also the patron saint of Italy, so it would be fun to provide refreshments with an Italian theme, such as amaretti and Garibaldi biscuits. A more elaborate meal involving pasta and gelati (ice cream) would be even greater fun.

* * *

St Luke

Date: 18 October

Web link

www.healthcaresunday.org.uk

Introduction

St Luke is the patron saint of doctors and health care workers because an early tradition suggests that he was a physician. His saint's day is an opportunity to support the activities of all who work in the health professions.

Key Bible verse

You, Lord God, bless everyone who cares for the poor, and you rescue those people in times of trouble.
PSALM 41:1

Bible links

- Colossians 4:14 (Luke is referred to as a 'dear doctor')
- Psalm 41 (God cares for those who look after people who are unwell)
- Matthew 4:23 (Jesus demonstrates the importance of healing people)
- Matthew 25:31–46 (Jesus says that people who tend those who are unwell are looking after him)

Key focus

Building community relationships; campaigning and social action

Key group

Church family; children

Activity ideas

Make sure that the medical professions are included in the intercessions at the nearest service to St Luke's Day, and invite everyone to send a card of thanks to any health workers known to them or to local surgeries, hospitals, hospices and nursing homes. Children's groups may wish to hold a session to make special cards to be distributed.

Another idea is to offer to provide some new toys for the waiting areas of some of these places. This is not an excuse for children to give away their cast-off toys, as these are likely to be battered and look tired. A better idea would be to take a few children to buy some suitable toys to give to the surgeries. The children will remember the special occasion as well as being able to offer their insights into what would be good purchases.

Prayer

Provide a large, plain box with a slit in the top. Decorate the front of the box with a red cross and provide paper and pencils. Invite people to write the names of those who work in the health professions, or the names of surgeries or research groups, on to the paper to be posted into the box. Make sure that the intercessions are offered in a service.

Developing the theme

'St Luke's Little Summer' is a name for the few days of late summery weather that often occur around 18 October. This could be just the time to have a follow-up session to any holiday club or event that the church ran during the summer. Print some of the photos or build them into a PowerPoint display for the event. Invite everyone back in their costumes or with any special crafts created for a 'Do you remember the bit when…' session. Sing the theme song or any particular chorus that was enjoyed during the original event. Share a meal and memories.

Build on the relationships. Children and families may find it easier to return for a 'bit more of the same' than to take part in a more traditional church service. Regular reunion events help to maintain links until the next holiday club or activity session takes place.

* * *

Apple Day

Date: 21 October

Web links

www.commonground.org.uk/appleday

Introduction

In recent years, 21 October has been adopted as National Apple Day. The charity Common Ground provides lots of community ideas to mark Apple Day.

You could use this secular day as a different way to approach Bible teaching about the importance of keeping God's commands. It also links with a late-medieval tradition that Calvary and paradise were on the same site, with the suggestion that pips from the apple that Adam ate grew into the tree from which the cross was made.

Key Bible verse

Keep me as the apple of your eye; hide me in the shadow of your wings.

PSALM 17:8 (NIV)

Bible link

- Proverbs 7:2 (NIV) (encourages us to treasure God's teachings)

Key focus

Providing sacred space for reflection; fun; fundraising for charity

Key group

Church family; schools; local community

Activity ideas

Mark the occasion by organising a Christian Apple Day activity session. Ideas for the day could include apple-dunking or bobbing. (Float apples in a big bowl of water or suspend them on string from a rail.) You could also taste segments of different types of apples. Talk about how the same kind of fruit can look and taste so different.

Make apple prints by cutting apples in half horizontally to show the star on the inside and dipping into paint. Talk about the hidden treasure that God has placed inside each of us.

Create a mural with an outline of an apple tree's trunk and branches, and invite everyone to cut out an apple shape on which to write their name and add to the tree.

Learn the carol 'Jesus Christ the apple tree'.

Serve Fairtrade apple juice, local apples, apple flapjack or muesli bars containing apple.

Invite an apple grower to talk about their craft.

Finally, use one of the following Bible verses as a memory verse:

- 'Keep me as the apple of your eye; hide me in the shadow of your wings' (Psalm 17:8, NIV)
- 'Keep my commands and you will live; guard my teachings as the apple of your eye' (Proverbs 7:2, NIV)

Prayer

Offer everyone an apple to hold during this 'apple' prayer. Ask them not to start eating it yet!

Ask God to direct your thoughts...
Praise him for the gift of so many delicious fruits we can enjoy...
Pray for people who work to grow the fruits we buy...
Listen to God as you sit quietly...
Enjoy all God's gifts that you can experience around you...

Encourage everyone to take the apple home to enjoy later.

Developing the theme

If there is a glut of cooking apples, arrange a baking session to make individual and family-sized apple pies or crumbles. Advertise them for sale in aid of a named charity. It may be possible to take orders in advance. If the desserts are sold 'fresh', persuade people to buy extra to store in their freezer. Otherwise, take individual-sized crumbles as presents for elderly people who live alone.

* * *

The Eve of All Hallows

Date: 31 October

Web links

www.helpforheroes.org.uk

Introduction

In recent years, churches have been much more active in offering alternative activities for children and families to the ghoulish, and often scary, pastimes of commercial Halloween. Many children are often frightened by images of monsters and ghosts, so it is important for churches to offer happier celebrations. An obvious theme is to celebrate the saints, the heroes of the Christian faith.

With older children, lead a discussion before the event about Halloween traditions, to consider how unnerving it is for elderly people to have strangers knocking on their door after dark.

Key Bible verse

God blesses those people who refuse evil advice and won't follow sinners or join in sneering at God.

PSALM 1:1

Bible links

- Psalm 1:1–3 (Christian heroes study the Bible)
- Psalm 15 (a description of a godly person, a saint)

Key focus

Sharing the Christian story; fundraising for charity; fun

Key group

Children; schools; local community; families

Activity ideas

Invite everyone to a Halloween Heroes party. Ask them to dress up as heroes (suggest firefighters, nurses and superheroes such as Spiderman, or encourage them to think of their own ideas). Organise a parade of heroes once everyone has arrived, and invite some of the children to talk about their choice of costume. Offer face-painting (with an uplifting theme). Play cooperative games such as those suggested in *Instant Games for Children* (see details on page 211). Serve fun refreshments such as the following (but avoid things offered under the Halloween theme at supermarkets).

- Saintly sausages
- Cheerful chips
- Positive pizza
- Superhero sandwiches
- Bravery biscuits

Tell a heartening story about a hero, such as Daniel in the lions' den. A funny version of this story can be found in *The Lion Storyteller Bible by* Bob Hartman.[4]

More ideas for celebration can be found in *Better than Halloween* by Nick Harding.[5]

— Prayer —

Mighty God, thank you for fun and friendship as we enjoy our Halloween Heroes party. Help us to be brave heroes every day. Amen

Developing the theme

Challenge schools, organisations and buinesses to have a 'Dress as a hero' day in aid of a charity such as Help for Heroes. Suggest that they invite a donation of £5 (£1 for pupils) for the privilege of wearing 'heroic' fancy dress. Explain that the church is organising the event as part of their Eve of All Hallows celebrations because saints are the heroes of the Christian faith.

* * *

All Saints' Day

Date: 1 November

Introduction

Saints can be described as the heroes of the Christian faith, the people whom Christians admire. Knowledge of the stories of many saints has declined, so this idea is a way of sharing why some people are remembered as Christian heroes.

Key Bible verse

God blesses those people who refuse evil advice and won't follow sinners or join in sneering at God.
PSALM 1:1

Bible links

- Psalm 1:1–3 (Christian heroes study the Bible)
- Psalm 15 (a description of a godly person, a saint)

Key focus

Sharing the Christian story; fundraising for charity

Key group

Schools; local community; families

Activity ideas

If the church has good relations with the shops, business and organisations in the area, organise a treasure hunt to find details of saints displayed in the windows of these places. In a small village, arrange to display the different saint posters in the front windows of homes that are visible to passers-by.

Research on the internet will reveal who are the patron saints of doctors, butchers, shopkeepers, dentists, florists, accountants, schools and so on. Prepare an A4 sheet with the names of the patron saint, plus details of what they are the patron saint of and why, to display in the window. Offer a small prize for both the adult and the child who spot the most saint posters displayed in the area. Distribute entry forms through the church, school and some busy shops.

Place a posting box for the returns in the church if it is open and easily accessible, or provide a collecting box in a shop. Give the address of a private house in a small village. Allow at least one week, including some of half-term if possible, for people to take part. Ask the local paper for publicity (a poster about a saint in a shop window will make a good photo for them) as well as advertising through the church or area magazine and school newsletter.

— Prayer —

Creator God, the source of all holiness, thank you for the example of your saints in history and today. Help us to live as trainee saints. Amen

Developing the theme

Invite the library to create a display on the theme of saints and offer to provide colouring sheets, with the outlines of stained-glass window images of saints to be decorated. Activity sheets with a word search including names of saints, and interesting facts about the lives of saints, could also be prepared for distribution.

* * *

All Souls

Date: 2 November

Web links

www.winstonswish.org.uk
www.penhaligonsfriends.org.uk
www.childbereavement.org.uk
www.roadpeace.org

Introduction

People often need help, and even permission, to grieve. Advice on how to support grieving children and families can be found from such excellent organisations as Winston's Wish, Penhaligon's Friends and Child Bereavement Trust. Alongside the assistance that families need in the acute phase of bereavement, churches can also help everyone to deal better with the concept of death and grief by offering regular occasions and opportunities for remembering those who have died. All Souls' Day provides an annual occasion for people to mourn and remember.

Key Bible verse

God blesses those people who grieve. They will find comfort!
MATTHEW 5:4

Bible links

- Isaiah 53:3 (the prophet predicted that God's chosen rescuer would experience grief and sorrow)
- Isaiah 61:2–3 (God instructs us to care for those who grieve)
- John 11:35 (Jesus wept when he mourned for his friend)

Key focus

Providing sacred space for reflection

Key group

Church family; schools; local community; families

Activity ideas

Advertise that the church will be open especially for everyone who wishes to remember or mourn those who have died. If possible, arrange for the opening to be between 2 and 8pm. This means that parents can call in before collecting children from school, older people can come along before it is dark, schoolchildren can visit after school and those at work can attend on their way home.

Ensure there are at least two people to welcome visitors gently to the church and to provide guidance about the various activities on offer. One of these stewards should be able to act as a chaplain. A simple sheet of instructions may be helpful, along with contact details of clergy and lay pastoral ministers as well as details of the websites of various organisations that can support those who grieve.

Light the candles on the main altar, if that is the custom of the church, but have the lighting level as low as is safe. Invite visitors to light a tealight candle in memory of the people they wish to remember. These could be placed on the aisle floor of the unlit chancel of the church so that, eventually, a spread of tealight candles will illuminate the area. (Provide wax tapers to help people to light their candle.) Say a simple prayer of thanksgiving and remembrance at half-hourly intervals, after announcing that it is going to take place.

Supply paper and pens for people to write prayers, trays of sand for people to finger as they reflect, and lengths of coloured ribbon or wool for people to add to a simple tapestry of remembrance. Make it clear that people are welcome to sit quietly and do nothing.

It may be helpful to provide a quiet area where no particular activity will take place. If the church has a memorial book, this should be available for visitors to look at.

One church, in partnership with the local school, offered every pupil the chance to write or draw their memories of someone who had died. All the work produced was gathered up and taken into the church and laid on the altar (the memories were not for public reading). The church was then open from straight after school and into the early evening, with hot chocolate, tea and cake on offer. All visitors were invited to light a tealight candle in memory of someone. These candles were positioned in the unlit chancel and built up into a moving display. The church ensured that there were people available to act as chaplains for those who were grieving.

— Prayer —

Sing quietly:

Be still and know that I am God (three times)
I am the Lord that healeth thee (three times)
In thee, O Lord, I put my trust (three times)

Developing the theme

The annual Day of Remembrance and Hope for Road Traffic Victims is observed on the third Sunday of November. Announce that the church will be open during, for example, the afternoon of that day for anyone who wishes to remember those who have been killed, or bereaved, by a road accident. Publicise a simple timetable of activities. This could include an hour of silence during which people are invited to light a candle in remembrance. Paper oak leaves, on which the name of the person to be remembered can be written, can be obtained from RoadPeace. All the prayers can be gathered and presented in a time of prayer or service that takes place towards the end of the afternoon. Provide refreshments, but do not be surprised if people choose not to stay.

* * *

Remembrance

Date: 11 November, and second Sunday in November

Introduction

The marking of Remembrance Day has revived in recent years. Many schools, offices and businesses encourage people to keep the two-minute silence. Many churches provide a formal service of Remembrance on the second Sunday of November, but there are also opportunities for more informal activities.

Key Bible verses

Your way is perfect, Lord, and your word is correct. You are a shield for those who run to you for help.

PSALM 18:30

God blesses those people who make peace. They will be called his children!

MATTHEW 5:9

Bible links

- Psalm 46 (God is strong and ready to help us)
- Psalm 62 (God is the mighty rock where we can find peace and safety)

Key focus

Providing sacred space for reflection; fundraising for the Royal British Legion

Key group

Church family; schools; local community; uniformed organisations

Activity ideas

Invite people to visit the church on Remembrance Day, or over the Remembrance weekend, to help create a memorial for all who have died in war-time. Suggest that they use one ribbon for each person they wish to remember. Provide 50cm lengths of wide red ribbon, tape or nylon 'kite' fabric. (It is also possible to use crêpe paper.) Erect a length of trellis to provide a framework to which the red material can be tied, or stretch thick string between posts to which the ribbons can be tied. Offer ribbon of another colour, such as white or black, so that people can also remember 'unknown' victims of war.

One church decided to invite people, including those who were passing by, to tie their red material on to the railings of the churchyard beside the main road. The youth group joined in by making huge poppies out of red crêpe paper stretched over thin wire frames. The activity was available for a focused period of time, 3–6pm.

Expand the opportunities for reflection by providing a poetry area. Display copies of a range of 'war' poetry for people to read. Suggested poems include the following.[6]

- Psalm 46
- 'The Soldier', Rupert Brooke
- 'Waste of Muscle, Waste of Brain', Geoffrey Studdert Kennedy
- 'The General', Siegfried Sassoon
- 'Everybody Sang', Siegfried Sassoon
- 'Spring 1942', Roy Fuller
- 'Hate', James Stephens

- 'Simplify Me When I'm Dead', Keith Douglas
- 'Last Post', Carol Ann Duffy

Also provide paper and pens for anyone who wishes to either write their own poem to add to the display or take home, or note down particular phrases that they have found helpful. If there is a war memorial inside the church building, offer an opportunity to light candles of remembrance in front of the monument or plaque.

— Prayer —

Give us, dear Lord, the courage to work for peace in our world, in our country, in our town, in our street, in our family, in our home, in ourselves.

Developing the theme

Provide a similar activity in school, either during an assembly or during the lunch break.

Many schools devote curriculum time to finding out about people who have served in the armed forces. Invite the school to display some of the work they produce in church over the Remembrance weekend.

* * *

11 Million Takeover Day

Date: early November

Web links

www.11million.org.uk/adult/11_million_takeover_day
www.childrenareunbeatable.org.uk

Introduction

Sir Al Aynsley-Green, the first Children's Commissioner, instituted a 'Takeover Day' in early November for the eleven million children and young people in this country. The aim is to encourage children to take over and to be in charge for the day. This not only encourages children to exercise responsibility, but also enables adults to learn from what children say and do when they are in charge.

Key Bible verse

He drags strong rulers from their thrones and puts humble people in places of power. God gives the hungry good things to eat, and sends the rich away with nothing.
LUKE 1:52–53

Bible links

- Isaiah 11:6–9 (the prophet's surprising vision of a topsy-turvy future)
- Isaiah 65:17–25 (the new creation)

Key focus

Campaigning and social action; fun

Key group

Church family; schools; families

Activity ideas

In schools, a child can take the place of the head teacher for the day, with the head teacher becoming a pupil in the child's class.

At church, ask children to come up with ideas for a 'takeover' in church on the nearest Sunday. These might include the following. However, it is important that children are given the opportunity to make suggestions, rather than being told what they are going to do!

- Children staying in church while the adults go out to the children's usual meeting space.
- Children giving the address or leading the intercessions.
- Children creating the flower arrangements or providing the music.

Some churches have revived the medieval 'Boy Bishop' tradition. At All Saints', Wellingborough, a 13-year-old boy was appointed to serve as a child bishop during Advent. He was provided with robes and regalia, and was blessed by the real bishop. He was asked to preach a sermon to the whole church, and he reported that he felt he had made a real difference. This has become a new, annual custom.

Another parish in the same diocese was so inspired by the concept of 'takeover' that they helped the children to appoint two child churchwardens to serve for a year, to represent the views of young people to the parochial church council.

— Prayer —

Surprising God, the Bible speaks of a future where the existing order is turned upside down. As we have fun doing things differently, with children and young people being in charge for a change, inspire us all to work for the coming of your kingdom where life will be better for everyone.

Developing the theme

The 'topsy-turvy' ideas of 'Takeover Day' fit very well with Christ the King day (see page 81). Some children, if they could take over power for a day, would want to do something to stop violence against children. The 'Children are Unbeatable' campaign works to ensure that children have equal rights to adults when it comes to being hit (at present, children and young people do not have the same protection as adults under the law).

* * *

World Toilet Day

Date: 19 November

Web links

www.worldtoilet.org
www.wateraid.org

Introduction

The World Toilet Organisation (WTO) exists to campaign about the global crisis in sanitation. A child dies somewhere in the world every minute, every day, because of poor sanitation. The WTO gives clear information about the scale of the problem as well as making it possible to donate a toilet for a family or school.

Key Bible verse

Can clean water and dirty water both flow from the same spring?
JAMES 3:11

Bible links

- Genesis 26:19 (Isaac's servants dug a well in Gerar valley and found fresh water)
- Ezekiel 34:18–19 (the importance of not having clean water or good pasture at the expense of other people)

- John 4:10 (God wants to give us water that brings life)
- Acts 4:32–34a (sharing what we have with others)

Key focus

Campaigning and social action; fundraising for charity

Key group

Church family; schools; local community; families

Activity ideas

Fundraising ideas to donate a toilet include providing a jar for everyone to take home, and asking them to donate a penny every time they 'spend a penny'. This idea could be shared with schools, shops or businesses. Create a sticky printed label for the jars, or small boxes, using the WTO logo. Include contact details for the church organising the collection, and the date when the campaign will close. Make a poster to accompany the jar so that everyone understands why the money is needed.

You could also organise a sponsored 'toilet sit', either on a borrowed, unattached lavatory (ask a plumber or builders' merchant to lend one) positioned somewhere very public or by using a single toilet cubicle. Make it clear that everyone will remain fully clothed at all times and that other lavatory facilities will be provided! Then invite volunteers to be sponsored to sit on the toilet for an hour. Organise a display of material about the global need for more sanitation so that visitors can see what they are helping. Make sure that the local media are invited to provide publicity. If a lavatory bowl can be borrowed from a local plumber or builder's merchant, you could position it at the back of the church and invite everyone to contribute small change by throwing it in. (Give people advance notice so that they know to bring some money to church.)

Again, this idea could be located in a school reception area with the permission of the head teacher.

— Prayer —

Creator God, thank you for the gift of clean water. Forgive us for not making sure that everyone has access to clean water and good sanitation. Help us to raise funds and to campaign for better facilities across the world. Amen

Developing the theme

In church, as a church family or as a children's project, find out as much as possible about World Toilet Day and hold a special all-age service based on the theme. In school, different year groups could be encouraged to explore the story of sanitation in this country and abroad. The work from this project could be linked to a special assembly on the theme. In both church and school, World Toilet Day could become an annual event.

Set up a focus area in church or school, containing pictures, facts and an opportunity for people to reflect and respond to the need for good sanitation both at home and overseas. People could write prayers based on their research and findings.

A good song to sing on this theme is 'Have you heard the raindrops (Water of life)'.

* * *

Prisons Week

Date: Third week of November

Web links

www.prisonsweek.org
www.amnesty.org.uk

www.prisonfellowship.org.uk
www.storybookdads.co.uk

Introduction

The aim is to pray for, and raise awareness of, the needs of prisoners and their families, victims of offenders, prison staff and all those who care.

Key Bible verse

The Lord God has told us what is right and what he demands: 'See that justice is done, let mercy be your first concern, and humbly obey your God.'
MICAH 6:8

Bible link

- Matthew 25:31–40 (Jesus tells his followers to look after people in prison)

Key focus

Campaigning and social action; fundraising for charity

Key group

Church family; local community

Activity ideas

Amnesty International has a 'Junior Urgent Action Network' to help children aged 7–11, with help from an adult, to be part of Amnesty's letter-writing campaigns about abuses of human rights. Children who join this network are not given graphic details of the violations, and Amnesty has a vigorous child protection policy to ensure that all material shared with children is appropriate for their age and level of understanding. Setting up an all-age Amnesty group is an exciting project for a church family that wants to take seriously Jesus' command to visit those in prison (Matthew 25:36).

November is a good time to launch such a project to link with both Prisons Week and the inclusion of Matthew 25:31–46 as the Gospel reading for Christ the King in Year A of the lectionary.

— Prisons Week Prayer —

Lord, you offer freedom to all people.
We pray for those in prison.
Break the bonds of fear and isolation that exist.
Support with your love prisoners and their families and friends,
prison staff and all who care.
Heal those who have been wounded by the activities
of others, especially the victims of crime.
Help us to forgive one another,
to act justly,
love mercy and walk humbly together with Christ in his strength
and in his Spirit, now and every day. Amen

Developing the theme

It is estimated that some 150,000 children in the UK have a parent in prison. The Prison Fellowship organises the Angel Tree programme to provide Christmas presents for the children of prisoners. Churches are needed to fundraise, buy and wrap gifts for this project, and Prisons Week is a good opportunity to launch local involvement.

Storybook Dads is another organisation that works to bridge the gap between parent and child when the parent is in prison. Prisoners are helped to record a bedtime story for their child on to a CD, so that children can share a story with their dad even when he is not there. This organisation also needs financial support.

* * *

Christ the King

Date: last Sunday before Advent

Introduction

This day is marked as the festival of Christ the King in many churches that follow the Common Revised Lectionary. Jesus is celebrated as the wise and eternal king who will bring justice to his people.

Key Bible verse

I will praise you, my God and King, and always honour your name.

PSALM 145:1

Bible links

- Psalm 93 (praising the Lord as king)
- Psalm 145 (God's kingly rule is eternal)
- Jeremiah 23:5–6 (God will appoint an honest king from the family of David)
- John 18:33–37 (Jesus and Pilate discuss whether he is a king)
- Romans 5:17 (because of Jesus we will live and rule like kings)
- Revelation 1:4–8 (Jesus is the king of all earthly kings)

Key focus

Sharing the Christian story

Key group

Church family; schools

Activity ideas

Set a large chair at the front (or on the chancel step) and invite everyone to decorate it to become a throne 'fit for a king'. (This could be the priest's chair, if you have one.) Provide tinsel, cushions, drapes, crêpe paper and so on. Discuss what is required to make the chair 'fit for a king'.

Invite a volunteer to come out to be a king. Dress them with a crown and a cloak, and give them some signs of wealth and power, such as a bag of chocolate coins. Sit them on the decorated throne. Invite out a second volunteer and then tell them they are going to be the king's servant. Provide them with a towel and apron and a bowl of water. Tell them they are to look after every need of the king—even washing his feet if necessary.

Explain that on this day we remember that the Jewish people were expecting a special king to be born, who would rule wisely and fairly. The prophet Jeremiah foretold how it would be.

Invite someone to read Jeremiah 23:5–6. Explain that the people were expecting a king who would sit on a throne (indicate the person playing the king on the throne), but that Jesus came as a servant. Ask the person playing the king to stand up and remove their royal outfit. Say that not only did Jesus leave his place in heaven but he also became a servant. Ask the person playing the king to take the towel, apron and bowl of water. Point out that, as odd as it may seem to think of a king taking a servant's role, it is even more amazing to think that Jesus, the king of heaven, sits us on the throne while he washes our feet.

Invite the person playing the servant to sit on the throne. Wonder aloud where is the best place for Jesus to be: sitting on the throne, or serving people and looking after them? Do not expect answers; leave the questions open.

If this activity is taking place in church, instead of the offering being taken in the usual way in the service, invite everyone to come out of their place to put their gift at the foot of the throne.

Songs that would be suitable for this activity include:

- O, Lord, all the world belongs to you
- King of kings, majesty
- Meekness and majesty (Tell everyone what the chorus is beforehand so that non-readers can join in)
- At the name of Jesus every knee shall bow
- My God is so big, so strong and so mighty (with actions!)

Prayer

Give everyone a paper crown[7] and a piece of plain paper towel (patterned would be distracting). Ask everyone to hold their crown and think about Jesus being the king. Pray for some of the places or situations where we would like Jesus to be the king, so that there might be peace and justice. Ask everyone to hold their paper towel and to think about how Jesus is asking each of us to be a servant in the world for him. Where is he calling us to serve? What would he like to see us helping with? Ask everyone to put on their crown. Explain that Paul tells us in his letter to the Romans (5:17) that 'God has been so kind to us, and he has accepted us because of Jesus. And so we will live and rule like kings.' Challenge everyone to think how we can share God's justice, love and peace in the world, if we are called to be kings like Jesus. Ask everyone to bring their crown and towel to lay before the chair that was decorated earlier as a throne, as they gather round to offer the prayers to God.

Developing the theme

This idea could be used for a school assembly either to mark Christ the King or in the week of Takeover Day (see page 73), but simplify the prayers to suit the number of children. For example, if the number of children assembled is fewer than 50, it is possible to provide them with a paper crown and towel, but it will take too long to hand out these items if there are more than 50 children present. In this instance, invite children to imagine holding a crown and a towel.

* * *

Buy Nothing Day

Date: Last Saturday in November

Web link

www.buynothingday.co.uk

See the ideas for keeping a 'Buy Nothing Day' given for Ash Wednesday on page 123.

Mission ideas for Winter (December, January and February)

The popular excitement about Christmas means that people are more likely to come to church in December than at any other time of year. Even families that would describe themselves as 'non-religious' may feel that they have not properly celebrated the Christmas holiday without an opportunity to sing carols or to watch a nativity play. When some school nativity productions include unusual extras such as fairies, space travellers and rock stars, it is important that churches ensure that the accurate story is shared as widely as possible. The season of Epiphany allows the church to continue teaching about Jesus' birth and early life into the new year.

The start of the new year is an opportunity for some people to reassess or realign their lifestyle. Churches are well placed to provide sacred space to reflect in this way. Ideas for mission during this season include projects such as campaigning for pure water throughout the world, promoting Fairtrade and supporting the work of schools and colleges in conjunction with Education Sunday.

Take-home gift from a crib or carol service

Date: December

Web link

www.barnabasinchurches/8065 (for download of story script)

Introduction

Many children may come to church in December for a school or church carol service, a Christingle or crib service, or another of the Christmas services. This provides an opportunity to tell children the account of the nativity and to give them a free gift to help build relationships. Hand out the bags as the children go home.

Key Bible verses

- Matthew 2:1–12 (the visit of the wise men)
- Luke 1:26–38 (Mary obeys Gabriel's message)
- Luke 2:1–20 (Jesus is born)

Key focus

Sharing the Christian story; providing sacred space for reflection; fun

Key group

Children; families; schools

Activity ideas

For each child, provide a small paper carrier bag with one each of the following items.[8] The story script gives the instructions for the child to follow, either reading it for themselves or as shared reading with an adult.

- Paper blower
- Feet picture
- Strip of cloth
- Cottonwool ball
- Party popper
- Star
- Paper crown
- Gold-covered chocolate coin
- Copy of the story script (downloaded from the Barnabas website)

Story script

In this bag you will find lots of interesting items to help you think about what happened at the first Christmas. Lay the items out in front of you in this order:

Paper blower
Feet picture
Strip of cloth
Cottonwool ball
Party popper
Star
Paper crown
Gold-covered chocolate coin

More than 2000 years ago, God began something new.
He sent Gabriel, one of his angels, to visit Mary. She was a teenager living in Nazareth. Gabriel had a message from God for Mary. *(Blow the paper blower.)*

'You will have a baby. You will call him Jesus. He will be the son of God.'

Mary was engaged to be married to Joseph. When the baby was nearly due to be born, they had to travel to Bethlehem to be counted in a census. *(Pick up the feet and think about walking a long way.)*

When they arrived in Bethlehem, they could not stay in the inn because there was no room for them. The baby was born and Mary laid him in a manger. *(Touch the cloth and imagine it wrapped around baby Jesus.)*

Meanwhile, there were some shepherds looking after their sheep in a field. *(Stroke the cottonwool ball and think about the sheep.)* An angel appeared in the sky and spoke to the shepherds. *(Blow the paper blower.)*

'Don't be afraid of me! Your Saviour has been born and you can find him in Bethlehem.'

Suddenly a huge band of angels appeared in the sky, praising God. 'Praise God in heaven!'

(Pull the party popper and imagine the angels in the sky.) The shepherds hurried to visit the new baby in Bethlehem and they were very excited.

A new star had appeared in the sky. *(Take the star and hold it high in the air.)* The star had been seen by some wise men from the east. *(Put on the paper crown and pretend to be one of the wise men.)* The wise men followed the star until it stopped just where baby Jesus was to be found. They brought special presents for Jesus: gold, frankincense and myrrh. *(Eat the chocolate coin as you think about what present you would like to bring to Jesus.)*

You may want to say this prayer: 'Be near me, Lord Jesus; I ask you to stay close by me for ever, and love me, I pray. Bless all the dear children in your tender care; prepare us for heaven, to live with you there. Amen.'

Have a very happy Christmas!

— Prayer —

Generous God, when so many people are weighed down with bags of Christmas shopping, may these bags which contain the story of the first Christmas and the birth of your son, Jesus, lighten the hearts of those who receive them.

Developing the theme

Rent a market stall or display space in a shopping centre for a single Saturday in December to hand out the goody-bags. Include an invitation to suitable church services, along with contact details for the church (including its website).

The story script could be used for a school assembly or school visit to church. Make up six bags with all the props, and script. Invite six children to come to the front to help you tell the story by using the props when you give them the signal. It would be good to end the time of collective worship by singing just the last verse of 'Away in a manger' so that children become aware that it is a prayer. Replenish the bags with fresh party poppers and chocolate coins so that the chosen children can play their way through the story again later.

* * *

Nativity from scratch

Date: December or early January

Web link

www.barnabasinchurches/8065 (for download of script)

Introduction

Nativity plays are always popular but they can take a long time to rehearse. This idea is for an instant play in which everyone can take part. For the performance you will need an overall leader, a narrator, a stage manager and someone in charge of music. These people need to rehearse the presentation before the event. They will then need to trust each other to react swiftly to any unforeseen happenings during the performance. During the performance, the leader will introduce and conclude the production, the narrator will read the Bible passages, the stage manager will announce the instructions in brackets and help to move people into place, and the music director will lead the carols on the stage manager's given signal.

Key Bible verses

- Isaiah 9:2, 6–7 (prophecy of a Saviour)
- Luke 1:26–38 (Gabriel visits Mary)
- Luke 2:1–5 (Mary and Joseph go to Bethlehem)
- Luke 2:6–7 (no room in the inn)
- Luke 2:8–20 (angels invite the shepherds to see Jesus)
- Matthew 2:1–11 (wise men follow the star to Jesus)
- Matthew 2:12, 16 (Herod kills the baby boys)
- Matthew 2:13–15 (Joseph takes Mary and Jesus to Egypt)

Key focus

Sharing the Christian story; fundraising through the offering

Key group

Church family; schools; families

Activity ideas

Invite everyone, children and adults alike, to come dressed as their favourite nativity character. Provide some headdresses made from tinsel (angels), teacloths or similar cloths (shepherds) and paper crowns (wise men) for anyone who arrives without a costume. Make it clear that people are also welcome who do not wish to dress up.

Explain that everyone has a part to play in this nativity play. Each named character or group will be called out to play their part and told where to stand and what to do. Everyone is needed to sing the carols, and some people may prefer to stay in their place to do this. Assure everyone that the aim is not to create a polished presentation but to allow everyone to feel part of the story.

Provide a large candle on a stand at the front, but ensure that it is carefully placed so that it will not be knocked over during all the moving around.

Opening prayer

If possible, dim the lights for the opening prayer and first reading.

Leader: Heavenly Father, take us now to Bethlehem to learn more about the birth of your Son, Jesus. May we share in the excitement of the first Christmas. Amen

Bible reading: Prophecy from Isaiah

Those who walked in the dark have seen a bright light.
(Light the candle)
And it shines upon everyone who lives in the land of darkest shadows...
A child has been born for us. We have been given a son who will be our ruler.
His names will be Wonderful Adviser and Mighty God, Eternal Father and Prince of Peace.
His power will never end; peace will last for ever.
He will rule David's kingdom and make it grow strong.
He will always rule with honesty and justice.
The Lord All-Powerful will make certain that all of this is done.
ISAIAH 9:2, 6–7

Turn the lights up full.

Carol: Soon and very soon we are going to see the king (sung twice)

Invite everyone who is playing Mary to sit at the front. Ask them to pretend to do cleaning. Ask those playing the angel Gabriel to stand by the altar, and then to come forward to greet Mary.

Bible reading: An angel appears to Mary

God sent the angel Gabriel to the Galilean village of Nazareth to a virgin engaged to... a man descended from David. His name was Joseph, and the virgin's name, Mary... Gabriel greeted her: 'Good morning! You're beautiful with God's beauty, beautiful inside and out! God be with you.' She was thoroughly shaken, wondering what was behind a greeting like that. But the angel reassured her, 'Mary, you have nothing to fear. God has a surprise for you: you will become pregnant and give birth to a son and call his name Jesus. He will be great, be called "Son of the Highest". The Lord

God will give him the throne of his father David; he will rule Jacob's house forever—no end, ever, to his kingdom.'

Mary said to the angel, 'But how? I've never slept with a man.' The angel answered, 'The Holy Spirit will come upon you, the power of the Highest hover over you; therefore, the child you bring to birth will be called Holy, Son of God... Nothing, you see, is impossible with God.'

And Mary said, 'Yes, I see it all now: I'm the Lord's maid, ready to serve. Let it be with me just as you say.' Then the angel left her.
LUKE 1:26–38 (*THE MESSAGE*)

Carol: Kum ba yah (three verses: Kum ba yah; someone's singing; someone's praying)

Ask those playing Gabriel to sit down and those playing Mary to stay by the carpet. Invite those playing Joseph or the donkey to join the Marys.

Bible reading: Mary and Joseph (and the donkey) go to Bethlehem

In those days Caesar Augustus issued a decree that a census should be taken of the entire Roman world. (This was the first census that took place while Quirinius was governor of Syria.) And everyone went to his own town to register. So Joseph also went up from the town of Nazareth in Galilee to Judea, to Bethlehem the town of David, because he belonged to the house and line of David. He went there to register with Mary, who was pledged to be married to him and was expecting a child.
LUKE 2:1–5 (NIV)

Send those playing Mary, Joseph and the donkey around the church in a procession during the singing of the following carol.

Carol: Little donkey

Ask for those playing the innkeeper to come to the front. Those playing Mary, Joseph and the donkey stand in front of the innkeeper(s). The innkeeper(s) turn them away, but point to a side aisle or space.

Bible reading: The innkeeper turns Mary and Joseph away but suggests they use the stable

(Send those playing Mary and Joseph to the side aisle and invite any stable animals to come to the front.) While they were there, the time came for the baby to be born, and she gave birth to her firstborn, a son. She wrapped him in cloths and placed him in a manger, because there was no room for them in the inn.

LUKE 2:6–7 (NIV)

Carol: Away in a manger (verses 1 and 2)

Invite all the shepherds and sheep to gather in another part of the church, possibly at the back.

Bible reading: The shepherds are surprised by angels

That night in the fields near Bethlehem some shepherds were guarding their sheep. All at once an angel came down to them from the Lord, and the brightness of the Lord's glory flashed around them. The shepherds were frightened. But the angel said, 'Don't be afraid! I have good news for you, which will make everyone happy. This very day, in King David's home town a Saviour was born for you. He is Christ the Lord. You will know who he is, because you will find him dressed in baby clothes and lying on a bed of hay.'

Suddenly many other angels came down from heaven and joined in praising God. *(Invite those playing angels to join you and lead them to the shepherds.)*

They said: 'Praise God in heaven! Peace on earth to everyone who pleases God.' *(Direct the angels to go back to their places.)*

After the angels had left and gone back to heaven, the shepherds said to each other, 'Let's go to Bethlehem and see what the Lord has told us about.' They hurried off and found Mary and Joseph, and they saw the baby lying on a bed of hay. *(Lead the shepherds and sheep to the side aisle to visit the holy family.)*

When the shepherds saw Jesus, they told his parents what the angel had said about him. Everyone listened and was surprised. But Mary kept thinking about all this and wondering what it meant.

LUKE 2:8–19

Carol: Silent night (verses 1 and 2)

Bible reading continues:

As the shepherds returned to their sheep, they were praising God and saying wonderful things about him. Everything they had seen and heard was just as the angel had said.

LUKE 2:20

Lead the shepherds and sheep back to their place with shouts of praise such as 'Hallelujah'. Then invite those playing wise men, pages, camels and so on to assemble at the back so that they can make a procession.

Bible reading: Wise men visit the baby

When Jesus was born in the village of Bethlehem in Judea, Herod was king. During this time some wise men from the east came to Jerusalem. *(Invite the wise men's procession to front.)*

[They] said, 'Where is the child born to be king of the Jews? We saw his star in the east and have come to worship him.' When King Herod heard about this, he was worried, and so was everyone else in Jerusalem. *(Invite those playing Herod to come to the front. If there are no volunteers, ask a willing adult to play the part and give them a paper crown to wear.)*

Herod brought together the chief priests and the teachers of the Law of Moses. *(Invite those playing a chief priest or teacher of the law to come to the front. If there are no volunteers, again ask a willing adult to play the part. Alternatively, ask everyone to imagine Herod consulting the priests.)*

[Herod] asked them, 'Where will the Messiah be born?' They told him, 'He will be born in Bethlehem, just as the prophet wrote, "Bethlehem in the land of Judea, you are very important among the towns of Judea. From your town will come a leader, who will be like a shepherd for my people Israel."' *(Send the priests and teachers to sit down. Ask Herod to turn to the wise men.)*

Herod secretly called in the wise men and asked them when they had first seen the star. He told them, 'Go to Bethlehem and search carefully for the child. As soon as you find him, let me know. I want to go and worship him too.' *(Invite those who wish to play the part of a star to come to the front. If there are no volunteers, have a star suspended from a rod and invite someone to walk in front of the wise men's procession to lead the way.)*

The wise men listened to what the king said and then left. And the star they had seen in the east went on ahead of them until it stopped over the place where the child was. They were thrilled and excited to see the star. *(The wise men's procession, led by the star, arrives at the stable area.)*

When the men went into the house and saw the child with Mary, his mother, they knelt down and worshipped him. They took out their gifts of gold, frankincense, and myrrh and gave them to him.

MATTHEW 2:1–11

Carol: We three kings (first and last verses)

Bible reading: Herod makes real trouble

Later they were warned in a dream not to return to Herod, and they went back home by another road... *(Send the wise men, camels and star back to their places.)*

When Herod found out that the wise men from the east had tricked him, he was very angry. He gave orders for his men to kill all the boys who lived in or near Bethlehem and were two years old and younger. This was based on what he had learnt from the wise men.

MATTHEW 2:12, 16

Carol: Unto us a boy is born (verses 1 and 3)

Invite those playing angels to go to the side aisle.

Bible reading: Mary, Joseph and Jesus head off to Egypt

After the wise men had gone, an angel from the Lord appeared to Joseph in a dream and said, 'Get up! Hurry and take the child and his mother to Egypt! Stay there until I tell you to return, because Herod is looking for the child and wants to kill him.' *(Send those playing Mary and Joseph to sit in another corner of the church, and ask the angels to return to their places.)*

That night, Joseph got up and took his wife and the child to Egypt, where they stayed until Herod died.

MATTHEW 2:13–15

Brief pause.

Conclusion: Explain that this is not the end of the story. When Jesus grew up he said...

Bible reading

I came so [all of you] can have real and eternal life, more and better life than [you] ever dreamed of.

JOHN 10:10 (*THE MESSAGE*)

Leader: Today, we are an important part of the continuing story of God's love for the world he created and for his people.

How can we show God's love to everyone during the seasons of Advent and Christmas? How would our lives change if we had the opportunity to visit Jesus lying in the manger?

Please will the people who played Mary and Joseph come back to the stable area. I invite everyone else to gather around the stable area with their service sheets to sing the last carol if you wish to do so. It is all right to remain in your seat if you prefer. The chorus of the carol has the words, 'O now carry me to Bethlehem to see the Lord appear to men', and so I invite you to imagine that is happening as we sing.

After we have sung the carol, there will be the opportunity for you to make an offering here in the stable area.

You may wish to announce that the offering will be given to a charity, such as The Children's Society.

Carol: See him lying on a bed of straw

— Closing prayer —

May the joy of the angels, the eagerness of the shepherds, the perseverance of the wise men, the obedience of Joseph and Mary, and the peace of the Christ child be ours this Christmas.

FROM *THE PROMISE OF HIS GLORY*

Developing the theme

Invite a class from the local school to create a nativity play from scratch. This could be done with the class visiting the church, or with church members organising the event in the school hall.

* * *

Candle cascade

Date: New Year's Eve (31 December)

Alternative dates: Epiphany (6 January); Candlemas (2 February)

Web link

www.gratefulness.org/candles

Introduction

Invite the community into church to light a candle of prayer for their hopes for the New Year.

Key Bible verse

I may be sitting in the dark, but the Lord is my light.

MICAH 7:8B

Bible links

- Psalm 119:105 (God's word gives light)
- Isaiah 9:2 (people who have been in darkness have seen a great light)
- Matthew 5:16 (let your light shine so that others may see your good deeds)
- John 1:5 (darkness cannot put out Christ's light)
- 1 John 1:5 (God is light and has no darkness in him)

Key focus

Providing sacred space for reflection; fun

Key group

Schools; local community; families

Activity ideas

This is a drop-in event. If it is planned for New Year's Eve, the event can be timed to take place in the late afternoon and early evening (between 4.30 and 7.30pm) so that it does not clash with New Year's Eve parties. It provides an opportunity for spiritual reflection on an occasion that many people consider significant.

Position one big lit candle at the front of the church and offer everyone the opportunity to light a tealight candle from it. Provide tapers to help with the lighting of the small candles. Invite visitors to place their tealight candle either around the front of the church or in a long line down the central aisle. (Where the tealight candles are displayed will depend on both a risk assessment and aesthetic inclination.) Unlit tealight candles could be arranged to mark out the digits of the new year, so that the date gradually becomes illuminated.

Have at least two people available as stewards to welcome visitors and to explain what to do. Make sure that a few initial candles have been lit before the opening time to create atmosphere. Play quiet music with the lights as low as is safely possible.

At each half-hour, offer public spoken prayer to gather up the thoughts and prayers represented by the candles. Give everyone a prayer card with a suggested prayer for them to use and take home.

Offer two or three prayer stations on the theme of light if there is space around the church. Ideas for prayer stations include the following.

- Draw or paint a large red flame on to a sheet of A3 black card or paper. Invite people to draw a picture of themselves on to a Post-it note to press on to the flame picture. Suggest that they think about where God would like them to share his light in the world. Provide plenty of pens to use.
- Supply sheets of newspaper and a waste bin. Invite people to find a story in the newspaper that needs God's light, then cut or tear out the report, scrunch it up and throw it in the bin. It may be easier to cut out possible stories in advance for people to browse through. Include plenty of pictures.
- Provide copies of the Bible in several versions, including those produced for children, and comfortable chairs or beanbags on which to sit. Display the words of Psalm 119:105 and suggest that people open one of the Bibles to find some of God's light.
- If internet access can be provided, invite people to light a 'cyber-candle' at the Gratefulness website.

— Prayer —

Send your light before us, Lord, into the new year, that we will not walk in darkness but in the brightness of your love.

Developing the theme

Another idea, if sufficient jars can be found, is to have the tealight candles lit inside jars that are displayed outside the church. This sort of event needs good publicity, such as candle-shaped invitation cards delivered to each house (including a phone contact so that housebound people can participate). Make sure that local toddler groups or pre-school nurseries are told about the occasion as this event would be popular with small children. The publicity should make it clear that everyone is welcome, whether they stay for an hour or just five minutes. The first publicity for this event could be an appeal for the donation of empty, clean jars to use.

As with Christingle services, it is advisable to inform the church insurance company that the event is taking place. One urban church that held such an event during Advent offered free hot chocolate to visitors. They were surprised by the number of passers-by who joined in because they saw the activity in the churchyard and heard music playing.

* * *

Living Epiphany

Date: 6 January

Introduction

Many churches, both urban and rural, have developed different forms of a 'living nativity' in which people and animals act out the Christmas story around their neighbourhood. The villages of Glaston and Bisbrooke in Rutland developed a 'living Epiphany' to mark the journey of the wise men and to provide a community activity after Christmas. Their aim was to enable everyone to play a part as they experienced the excitement and mystery of the journey to Bethlehem.

Key Bible verse

When Jesus was born in the village of Bethlehem in Judea, Herod was king. During this time some wise men from the east came to Jerusalem.
MATTHEW 2:1

Bible links

- Matthew 2:1–12 (the visit of the wise men)

Key focus

Sharing the Christian story; providing sacred space for reflection; fun

Key group

Church family; local community; families

Activity ideas

Gathering

Meet in a hall or home some way away from the church and make the following items.

- A single large star to carry at the head of the subsequent procession.
- Paper crowns for everyone to wear.[9]
- A decorated gift box for each person (to save time, cut out the gift boxes in advance so that they are ready to decorate and assemble).[10]

Reading

Read the first part of the account of the visit of the wise men to Jesus, from Matthew 2:1–8.

Reflection

Invite everyone to think about an imaginary gift that they would like to put in their box to take to Jesus' crib. This could be a talent, such as cooking; a virtue, like kindness; or a practical object.

Song

We three kings of Orient are

Journeying

Walk in procession around the neighbourhood, following the star carried by the leader of the group. It would be fun to use satellite navigation to give directions to each house in turn, provided that they are far enough apart. Ensure that the route is suitable for baby-buggies, wheelchairs and those who are unsteady on their feet.

Pause

Stop at three or four prearranged homes to knock and ask if this is where the baby born to be king of the Jews can be found. At each halt, sing a suitable hymn or song, such as one of the following.

- I want to see your baby boy
- Riding high and low
- O come, let us adore him
- As with gladness men of old
- The first nowell
- The virgin Mary had a baby boy

Invite everyone to join in to give a blessing to the home with the words, 'May Christ bless this house'. If the householders are willing, chalk 20+C+M+B+the last two digits of the year over the lintel of the doorway (or have them printed and laminated on a strip of card to affix with Blu-tack). The C, M, and B can stand for the traditional names of the three wise men, Caspar, Melchior and Balthasar, or they may be taken to stand for *Christus Mansionem Benedicat* (the words of the blessing in Latin).

Arrival

The final destination is the church, which represents Bethlehem. If possible, arrange for a family with a new(ish) baby to be waiting in the church to meet everyone when they arrive.

Worship

Read the end of the account of the visit of the wise men, from Matthew 2:9–12. Invite everyone to offer their gift boxes at the crib.

— Prayer —

Lord God, as we offer our talents and best thoughts to your Son, we pray that you will bless all of us who have taken part in today's journey. Bless our homes and all who live there. As we leave this place, may we be a blessing to other people. We ask this in the name of Jesus. Amen

Song

Sing a song or hymn such as 'Come on and celebrate', 'In the bleak midwinter' or 'What child is this?'

Receiving

Offer everyone a Jelly Baby to represent Jesus' birth, a chocolate coin to stand for the visit of the wise men to Bethlehem, and a mini-egg to remind everyone that the story of Christmas continues to Easter. These items can be placed in the gift boxes to be taken home.

Refreshments

In Mexico, it is traditional to bake a crown-shaped cake to serve with a drink of hot chocolate. A simple, plain cake would be just as welcome but it may be possible to include a single cherry in the mix before it is baked, or carefully to insert one into a shop-bought cake. When the cake is cut, the person who receives the cherry in their slice receives a special prize.

Developing the theme

Invite everyone to attend in fancy dress, if they wish. Some may come as wise men or Herod. They could also dress as priests or servants. If there are people who are willing to act, the wise men's visit to Herod's palace could be re-enacted, complete with consultation of the chief priests and teachers of the law.

* * *

Campaign for clean water

Date: Third Sunday of Epiphany

Web links

www.pottersforpeace.org
www.wateraid.org
www.worldwatercouncil.org
www.tearfund.org

Introduction

In the Year B lectionary readings for the third Sunday of Epiphany, the Gospel focuses on the first miracle, Jesus turning water into wine. This is a good time to highlight the work of Potters for Peace (see page 214 for further information), an organisation that works to process dirty water into clean water. Information can also be gathered from Water Aid, the World Water Council and Tearfund.

The provision of pure, clean drinking water must seem like wine, and a miracle, for those who have lived with inadequate water supplies. Every year there are 1.7 million deaths, mainly of children under the age of five, from diarrhoea caused by poor water. The UN's Millennium Development Goal is to halve the number of people unable to reach or afford safe drinking water by the year 2015. Diseases related to inadequate water and sanitation cause an estimated 80 per cent of all sickness in the developing world.

Key Bible verse

Jesus told the servants to fill [the jars] to the top with water.
JOHN 2:7

Bible links

- John 2:1–11 (Jesus turns water into wine)
- John 4:10 (God wants to give us water that brings life)
- James 3:11–12 (the importance of having a clean well to provide fresh water)

Key focus

Campaigning and social action; fundraising for charity

Key group

Church family; school; local community

Activity ideas

Challenge everyone who usually buys bottled water to fill an empty bottle with tap water to use for just one day. Ask them to donate the money they have saved to Potters for Peace,[11] Water Aid or Tearfund.

Set a target for fundraising within the group, such as £50 to fund a hand pump through Wateraid. Publicise this target amount and challenge everyone to think about how much they spend each week on bottled water or on buying drinks in a pub or coffee shop. Then ask everyone to make a donation.

Offer families an empty water bottle to fill with their small change as they give thanks for the gift of fresh water. Set a date, about two weeks away, for the bottles to be returned full of coins and the money to be counted. Take photographs of the organisers holding empty water bottles ready to be filled, and send them, with a press release explaining what is going to happen, to the local press. It may be possible to borrow a sample hand pump from a local water company to include in the photos.

— Prayer —

Creator God, thank you for the gift of living water. Help us to campaign so that everyone can have fresh water to drink.

Developing the theme

Persuade a local pub or coffee shop to place an empty water bottle on the counter and invite their customers to donate any small change that will fit through the neck to the chosen charity.

Encourage people to email or write to the government to press for progress on the Millennium Goal to increase the availability of safe drinking water. Instructions to do this can be seen on the Water Aid website.

* * *

Holocaust Memorial Day

Date: 27 January

Web links

www.holocaustmemorialday.gov.uk
www.hmd.org.uk
www.gratefulness.org/candles

Introduction

27 January is the date of the anniversary of the liberation of the concentration camp at Auschwitz-Birkenau in 1945. The date has been chosen as the occasion to remember all victims of genocide, not just in the Second World War but also in Bosnia, Cambodia, Darfur and Rwanda. Many schools mark the occasion with a special assembly, and many local authorities make provision for formal memorials.

Key Bible verse

God blesses those people who make peace. They will be called his children!

MATTHEW 5:9

Bible link

- Psalm 133 (The value of living in harmony)

Key focus

Providing sacred space for reflection

Key group

Schools; local community

Activity ideas

In the church, create a display of photographs and information about the Holocaust or one of the more recent genocides and invite the local community to visit. This can be done by contacting the local press and radio station, as well as by posters and leaflets and personal contacts. Provide a number of ways for people to respond to what they see, such as the following ideas.

- Provide a large, clear bowl of water and a supply of sugar cubes. Invite people to place a single sugar cube into the bowl of water, and to pray that God will take away some of the anger and violence in the world as they watch it dissolve.
- Supply tealight candles and tapers for people to light from a larger candle. Display a copy of the proverb 'It is better to light a candle than to curse the darkness'.
- Provide one large sheet of paper with the outline of the word 'war' written across it and another with the word 'peace'. Encourage people to write or draw prayers on to each outline.
- Ask people to draw a small self-portrait around the border of a large sheet of paper on which Psalm 133:1 is written ('It is truly wonderful when relatives live together in peace').
- If internet access can be provided on a laptop, offer visitors the opportunity to light a virtual candle with their prayer for peace or for the victims of genocide, on www.gratefulness.org/candles
- Provide kosher sweets if the Holocaust has been the main focus of the display.[12] Otherwise, offer edible treats from the appropriate culture, such as dates and figs for Bosnia.

— Prayer —

Father of all, it is truly wonderful when your people live together in harmony. Help us to remember the terrible crimes that have been committed against huge groups of people, even in recent years. We pray for all those who mourn or continue to live in fear. Inspire us to work for peace in our own community and across the world.

Developing the theme

Contact the local school to offer assistance with their own plans. They may be glad to be able to bring a class of pupils to experience the display and activities in the church.

* * *

Education Sunday

Date: Ninth Sunday before Easter

Web link

www.educationsunday.org

Introduction

Education Sunday has been observed since 1878, to celebrate the achievements of educational work and to pray for all who work, as staff or students, in education. It covers schools and nurseries, colleges and universities. Alongside these formal educational establishments, we are all called to share our faith with the following generations.

Key Bible verse

Come, my children, listen as I teach you to respect the Lord.
PSALM 34:11

Bible link

- Psalm 78:5–7 (teaching the next generation about God's love)

Key focus

Providing sacred space for reflection; campaigning and social action

Key group

Church family; schools; local community

Activity ideas

Churches Together in England provide annual material to mark Education Sunday for use in worship. This is available from the Education Sunday website.

Churches can also mark the occasion by approaching nurseries, pre-schools, schools and colleges for prayer requests. Use any existing links to do this. For example, if a school or college has used the church building for a Christmas carol service, approach the same person who organised that event. Alternatively, ask members of the congregation if they already have a link with one of the institutions as a parent, employee or volunteer. Even if such an approach is too difficult to arrange, pray for as many of the educational institutions as possible on Education Sunday and then deliver a card indicating that the school or nursery, including all the people involved in its work, was prayed for by name.

— Prayer —

Thank you, God, for all the people who work in schools.
Education is a precious gift, so help us not to waste opportunities to learn.
Also, we ask that schools may be safe and welcoming places for everyone.
Choose people to work as teachers and support staff.
Help everyone to receive the education they need, particularly in poorer countries.

Developing the theme

Encourage families to pray by name for everyone who teaches, or has taught, members of their own family.

* * *

St Valentine's Day

Date: 14 February

Introduction

This date has become the first commercial marketing opportunity in the calendar, filling shop shelves between the January sales and Mothering Sunday (Mother's Day). It has also assumed huge importance for everyone, including small children, to celebrate in some way. This is an opportunity for churches to challenge the prevailing culture.

Key Bible verses

God is love. If we keep on loving others, we will stay united in our hearts with God, and he will stay united with us.

1 JOHN 4:16

My dear friends, we must love each other. Love comes from God, and when we love each other, it shows that we have been given new life. We are now God's children, and we know him.
1 JOHN 4:7

Key focus

Providing sacred space for reflection; building community relationships

Key group

Church family; local community

Activity ideas

Hand out small Fairtrade chocolate and biscuit bars to passers-by in the street. Try to have several people taking part in the giveaway. Place a small sticker on each bar with the words, 'A small gift of love to mark St Valentine's Day, with best wishes from [name of your church]'. Focus the activity on one of the following areas.

- Outside the church building if it is on a main thoroughfare during the morning or evening rush hour.
- Outside the school gate at going home time (but ask permission from the head teacher).
- By a bus stop or at a train station (again, ask permission if you will be standing on their property).
- Outside a sports venue if there is a major event that day.
- Ask permission to provide a box of confectionery for any residential home in the area, with sufficient for staff and residents to share (check that what you plan to provide will be suitable for them to eat).

Take care not to damage anyone's business by standing outside a shop or stall that sells similar confectionery.

— Prayer —

Father God, your love for us existed before the world.
Lord Jesus, you showed your love for us by dying on the cross.
Holy Spirit, you have given us the power to love our neighbours as ourselves.

Developing the theme

Vanni Cook, a member of St Eustachius' Church in Tavistock, Devon, invited adults and children to write a four-line poem with no more than ten words in each line, on the theme of love, to celebrate St Valentine's Day. The poems were printed out to be uniform in format. They were laminated for display along the ledges of the pews and up the pillars in the church. Vanni received 1168 poems, far more than the 688 she aimed for, not just from Tavistock but from right round the world (showing what good publicity can achieve). The poems were published in an anthology, and the 'Poetry in the Pews' team members were amazed to receive funding for the event from the local council.

* * *

Fairtrade fortnight

Date: usually the last week of February and the first week in March

Web link

www.fairtrade.org.uk

Introduction

Even if your church already provides a Fairtrade stall after worship, Fairtrade fortnight is an opportunity to demonstrate that the church supports fair trade by joining in local events alongside the national annual campaign.

Key Bible verse

You must defend those who are helpless and have no hope. Be fair and give justice to the poor and homeless.

PROVERBS 31:8–9

Bible link

- Luke 4:18 (good news for the poor)

Key focus

Campaigning and social action; fun

Key group

Church family; families; local community; school

Activity ideas

Organise a cookery event for children, or children and adults together, using as many Fairtrade products as possible. Basic cupcakes are fun, and they can be elaborately decorated. Help everyone to weigh or spoon out their ingredients and mix them. A simple recipe can be found on page 209, together with a list of possible Fairtrade ingredients.

Everyone should be helped to make at least two cupcakes. Spoon the mixture into paper cases and bake in a moderate oven

(180°C/350°F/Gas Mark 4). Cupcakes can be cooked in a portable microwave oven if a traditional oven is not available.

Play some cooperative games, such as Fruit Salad (see page 205) or with a small parachute, while the cakes cook and cool. Then provide fresh icing and some toppings so that the cupcakes can be decorated. Finally, invite everyone to sit down to enjoy one of their cakes along with a drink—and take the other one home.

Another recipe for everyone to cook together is pizza. Offer Fairtrade tea, coffee and hot chocolate, or the chance to make smoothies with Fairtrade fruit. If the meeting space does not have a suitable oven, make bread-dough for everyone to take home in a food-grade plastic bag, along with baking instructions. A third option would be to make fruit salad by peeling, chopping and cutting up Fairtrade bananas, mangoes, pineapple, apple and citrus fruits.

Prayer

Give everyone a small Fairtrade banana. Hold the banana and thank God for all the people who were involved in growing, transporting, distributing and selling it. Open the neck of the banana and praise God for the richness of his creation. Peel the banana and pray for people with few rights and no 'voice'. Taste the banana and remember that God is good. Eat the banana and pray for all the people who will not have enough to eat today.

Developing the theme

Hold a Fairtrade supper for families, making sure that as many of the ingredients are fairly traded as possible. Provide a menu card that indicates which of the ingredients are Fairtrade. Show one of the Fairtrade films available from the Fairtrade Foundation. Have an intermission for a Fairtrade chocolate tasting so that everyone can vote for their favourite Fairtrade chocolate product.

Alternative ideas include providing a Fairtrade tuck shop at all midweek events run by the church for whatever age, or helping older children to provide a Fairtrade stall at school during a morning break or lunchtime. (Help them to negotiate permission, as well as to order the stock.) You might also consider helping children and young people to get their school registered as a Fairtrade School (if it isn't already) and assisting the local pre-school or nursery to do the same. Finally, you could provide a gift box of Fairtrade snacks for local schools, surgeries, residential homes or even businesses.

* * *

Bonus Day

Date: 29 February

Introduction

Leap years only come around every four years, so 29 February is a bonus. Many businesses and organisations encourage their employees to use the day to do volunteer work. This fits with the biblical concept of 'jubilee' in Leviticus.

Key Bible verse

You are like light for the whole world. A city built on top of a hill cannot be hidden, and no one would light a lamp and put it under a clay pot. A lamp is placed on a lampstand, where it can give light to everyone in the house. Make your light shine, so that others will see the good that you do and will praise your Father in heaven.

MATTHEW 5:14–16

Bible links

- Psalm 46:10 (be still to learn about God)
- Matthew 5:13 (be like salt for the community)

Key focus

Providing sacred space for reflection; campaigning and social action

Key group

Church family; families

Activity ideas

Take up any opportunities offered by an employer or school to work as an unpaid helper, or arrange to volunteer somewhere for an hour after work. Otherwise, determine to do as many acts of kindness as possible during the day. For example, you could:

- Let other people go ahead of you in a queue.
- Pick up some litter.
- Hold open a door for someone in a wheelchair or pushing a buggy.
- Pray for any telephone caller, after the call has ended.
- Spend time with someone who is housebound.
- Donate the free item from any 'buy one, get one free' purchases to a soup kitchen, refuge or family on a very low income.

— Prayer —

Generous God, help us to use our bonus time wisely—not for our own selfish pursuits, but for the good of those in need and for your glory.

Developing the theme

Use at least some of this bonus time as Sabbath time to spend quietly listening to God. Families could decide to have a 'no screens' evening to spend time together, going without television, computer or play screens on this unusual day.

Mission ideas for Spring (March, April and May)

As the days lengthen, many people have a little more energy and may be ready to try new things. The season may even lead them to 'Attempt great things for God and expect great things from God' (William Carey).

In the Christian calendar, spring is associated with the keeping of Lent, Holy Week and the celebration of Easter. This pattern provides valuable occasions to share the Christian story and to offer opportunities to reflect, particularly on Good Friday and at Easter. Ascension and Pentecost provide further points in the Christian year to share with the community.

Alongside this, the nation celebrates Mother's Day with enthusiasm, so there is an opportunity for churches to welcome families to a joyous Mothering Sunday occasion.

World Book Day always creates interest in schools and the media, and churches can find ways to join in the fun. Finally, Christian Aid week is an opportunity to find creative ways to help the local community to fundraise.

Ash Wednesday and Lent

Date: usually from the end of February and through March

Web links

www.buynothingday.co.uk
www.micahchallenge.org.uk
www.simplify.org.uk

Introduction

This first day of Lent is an opportunity to challenge people to reflect on the way they live and to invite them to consider living more simply, at least for the duration of the season. Many people are familiar with the idea of giving up something for Lent, and these ideas link with national campaigns such as National No Smoking Day.

Key Bible verse

Why waste your money on what really isn't food? Why work hard for something that doesn't satisfy?

ISAIAH 55:2A

Bible links

- Ecclesiastes 5:10–12 (money is not the answer to everything)
- Isaiah 58:6–8 (the worship God wants is for us to feed those who are hungry, share our homes with those in need and give clothes to people who need them)
- Matthew 6:1 (do good deeds but do not show off)
- Matthew 6:24 (it is impossible to serve both God and money)

Key focus

Providing sacred space for reflection; campaigning and social action; fundraising for charity

Key group

Church family; schools

Activity ideas

Challenge older children, perhaps through school and families, to have a Buy Nothing Day. Ash Wednesday, or a Friday in Lent, would be a good day for a fast from spending. This would mean that discussion about the concept should take place at least the weekend beforehand.

Ideas include inviting everyone to note down everything they have spent over the previous 24 hours and then discussing how much of this expenditure is essential. Remind people that nearly a third of the world's population—two billion people—live on less than £1 per day. If you can provide live internet access, invite people to look at the Simplify website from the Evangelical Alliance, which encourages everyone to live small but think big.

Next, get everyone to talk about how they would get through an ordinary day if they had no money in their pocket. In pairs, encourage everyone to plan how they will manage to buy nothing on the chosen day. Remind them that they are not allowed to borrow money from anyone else or ask others to pay for them. Pray for everyone taking part to have the commitment to carry out their plan. Finally, discuss whether participants should pledge to give half or all the money they will not have spent to a famine relief or development charity.

The Micah Challenge website focuses on the progress being made towards the Millennium Development Goals and how individuals and churches can support the campaign.

Some people may choose to reschedule their weekend so that the week's food shop will take place on the Saturday instead of the preceding Friday evening, while others may forego a regular visit to the cinema or swimming pool. Others will find that they cannot meet their commitments without spending some money. The value of the event is in thinking through essential expenditure, such as a bus fare to visit a relative in hospital, and enjoyable but non-essential expenditure, such as a visit to a coffee shop.

The official Buy Nothing Day takes place on the last Saturday of November (see page 84), but its ideals fit well in Lent. The challenge can always be repeated later in the year.

— Prayer —

Father of all, help us to remember that everything we possess is a gift from you. We don't want to be greedy but we are not good at remembering how much others have to live without. Forgive us.

Developing the theme

A twelve-hour fast is a suitable challenge for young people aged ten and over, as long as they have permission from their parents or carers. Invite them to a day of activities between 8am and 8pm on a Saturday or Sunday. Get a specific consent form signed by parents or carers for this activity, indicating that the young people will only be given water to drink during the fast. Make sure to check what arrangements must be made for anyone with diabetes, or other health difficulties, to take part. Plan a range of activities to keep everyone busy, but ensure that some of the activities are restful, such as watching a DVD, so that not too much energy is used up. At the end of the day, plan a simple feast to mark the end of the fast.

Some people take the view that it is wrong to suggest to young people that fasting and restricting the intake of food always has spiritual benefits. The rise of eating disorders means that great care must be taken in this area. If you are concerned about this, another way to experience 'fasting' would be to run a similar day but to provide plain boiled rice and water in place of the extravagant meals that many of us regularly eat. Give a clear explanation that millions of people exist on such a plain diet.

* * *

World Book Day

Date: first Thursday in March

Web links

www.worldbookday.com
www.bookaid.org
www.bookstart.co.uk
www.careforthefamily.org.uk
www.christianmarketplace.org.uk
www.thereadingclub.co.uk
www.speakingvolumes.org.uk

Introduction

World Book Day (WBD) is promoted by UNESCO to encourage reading. It is celebrated in over 100 countries across the globe. In this country, schools and pre-schools can register to receive a £1 book token to give to each child. These can be exchanged for a special £1 WBD book or towards the cost of their own choice of book.

Key Bible verse

God made the four young men clever and wise. They read a lot of books and became well educated.

DANIEL 1:17

Bible link

- Ecclesiastes 12:12 (there are so many books)

Key focus

Building community relationships; campaigning and social action

Key group

Children; families

Activity ideas

Most schools and pre-schools are likely to be registered to receive the World Book Day vouchers, but many toddler groups do not realise that they are eligible. Check with the toddler group's leader to find out whether they have registered, and then offer to arrange it for them by visiting the website.

Offer to give toddler and play groups a gift of Christian books to add to their library to mark World Book Day. The Speaking Volumes charity provides packs of books at 50 per cent of the recommended retail price. Their selected packs include books for children's groups aged 0–5, for primary school children aged 5–11, and for teenagers.

Bookstart is a national programme that encourages parents and carers to enjoy books with children from as early an age as possible. Free books are provided for babies, toddlers and pre-school children through Bookstart coordinators. Contact the local Bookstart coordinator to get involved in the scheme—they may welcome the opportunity to visit a church-run toddler group.

A slightly different scheme is offered by Care for the Family. This charity provides a box of their own easy-to-read books that encourage people in everyday life, including parenting, marriage and money management. The idea is to display the books at meetings of toddler groups, or any other occasion when parents gather. These occasions might include waiting to collect children from a session of a uniformed group or a midweek club, for example. Parents and carers are encouraged to borrow the books for free. This mini lending library can be expanded with multiple copies once the most popular subjects have been identified.

— Prayer —

As we open a book, we thank you, God, for the creativity of authors and the hard work of those who produce books. Open our eyes, Jesus, to read books with your eyes. Open our minds, Holy Spirit, to understand books with your insight.

Developing the theme

Churches could expand the small lending library idea, to provide a range of Bibles and Christian storybooks, for children attending any church club or activity to borrow. The Speaking Volumes scheme can be used to provide basic stock. Local Christian booksellers will be happy to advise on a suitable range of books to purchase, and may be willing to negotiate a discount if a large number of books are being purchased. The Christian Marketplace website provides reviews of recently published books to assist in the selection process.

Another idea is to start a book group for older children, young people or adults. This could be a natural evening development for parents and carers bringing children to a group for tots or a toddler service. Alternatively, offer it as an after-school club as part of the Extended Schools programme. Choose current fiction and books on which new films have been based, rather than Christian material, and allow the discussion to raise points of interest to which Christian members can give their own perspective (but not using it as an opportunity to 'correct' the views of others).

For adults, advertise in the local community and hold a book group in a home, a local coffee shop or a pub. Keep refreshments simple: many book groups enjoy a glass of wine and small snacks as they chat. Arrange for one person in turn to lead the discussion on the current book. Make sure that members who do not attend church are given an equal chance to take on this role. Build relationships, have fun and make friends. Keep it as simple as possible: advice on setting up a book club can be found at The Reading Club website.

Finally, National Bookstart day is in October, so some of these ideas could be used in the autumn.

* * *

Red Nose Day

Date: middle of March

Web links

www.rednoseday.com
www.biblegateway.com

Introduction

Red Nose Day (RND) takes place every other year to raise money for people in need in both Africa and the United Kingdom. The event provides a good opportunity for Christians to support the fundraising efforts of the local community, or for them to take a lead in organising a fun occasion.

Key Bible verse

Very old people with walking sticks will once again sit around in Jerusalem, while boys and girls play in the streets.

ZECHARIAH 8:4–5

Bible links

- Jeremiah 31:4 (we are so precious to God that he will rebuild society so that we can play and dance)
- Matthew 5:13 (be like salt for the community)
- Mark 12:31 (love other people)

Key focus

Fundraising for charity; fun

Key group

Church family; children; schools; local community

Activity ideas

Invite people to come to the Sunday service wearing something red. Invite a donation to RND. Ask everyone to attempt to hold hands around the outside of the church to see if the building can be captured in a 'ring of red'. Smaller congregations, or those with particularly large buildings, could identify an area inside the building to capture inside the 'ring of red'.

Another idea is to arrange a Bible quiz in which all the answers to the questions feature the words 'red' or 'nose'. Use a Bible search engine to identify verses that include these key words to create the questions. This could be the basis of a quiz night, with people paying to take part, or a paper challenge which people have to buy to enjoy. Offer small prizes, and include a colouring competition so that the smallest children can also take part.

— Prayer —

Father of all, thank you for the fun of Red Nose Day. Thank you for the fun ways people think of to raise money. Thank you for the opportunity to share our money with people who need help.

Developing the theme

If a local organisation is arranging a quiz or fashion show, or something similar, in aid of RND, organise a church outing to take part.

* * *

Mothering Sunday

Date: the fourth Sunday of Lent, usually in March

Web links

www.careforthefamily.org.uk
www.childrenssociety.org.uk
www.themothersunion.org

Introduction

Mother's Day has become a huge and commercial occasion. There is plenty of opportunity for churches to offer a chance to reflect on family life.

Key Bible verse

'Respect your father and mother. And love others as much as you love yourself.'
MATTHEW 19:19

Bible link

- Exodus 20:12 (respect your father and mother)

Key focus

Sharing the Christian story; providing sacred space for reflection; fun

Key group

Church family; children; families

Activity ideas

Organise a short craft session on the day before Mothering Sunday, or after school the previous week (either at the school or on church premises). Remember that some children may come to this session but not to a Sunday service, so allow them to take home anything they make. Ideas for the session include the following.

- Create a large collage with a floral design to use as a banner or altar frontal for the service on Mothering Sunday.
- Make three-strand plaits using metre lengths of 10mm curling ribbon[13] in different spring colours. These can be used to decorate the ends of the pews or rows of chairs for the service. Many children will need to be taught how to plait (a fun activity in itself), and may wish to plait a friendship bracelet made of wool to take home.
- Decorate ready-made cupcakes with icing, and then offer a selection of sugar flowers, icing and chocolate sprinkles, wafer decorations, tubes of coloured icing to pipe shapes and so on.[14] Everyone decorates two cakes, one for themselves and one for their mum or any special person who looks after them like a mum. Remember that boys may not want to use shades of pink on their cake, so offer a choice of colours, and possibly some football or superhero motifs.
- Decorate food-grade paper bags as wrapping to carry home the special cupcakes. Provide food decorating or non-toxic pens.

- If the session is the day before Mothering Sunday, help the children to make up a posy for their mum or special person. If possible, provide a selection of spring flowers, not just daffodils, so that children can add an anemone or primrose to their posy. If supplies of flowers are limited, invite everyone to choose three flowers and one piece of greenery.
- Offer children the opportunity to make a greeting card for their mother or grandmother. They may already have done this at school or in another group, so do not regard this as the main activity of the session.

Provide a time for reflection towards the end of the session. Gather everyone into a circle to listen to a Bible story such as Hannah taking Samuel to live with Eli, or Mary taking Jesus to the Passover festival. Read from a children's Bible (see page 210). Sit quietly for a few moments and then offer a prayer.

— Prayer —

God of love, thank you for all the people who look after us. Mums and grans and carers have to work so hard. Help us to help them when they need it.

Developing the theme

The Mothers' Union provides programmes throughout the world to improve parenting skills and to campaign against early marriage, child abuse and genital mutilation. Invite families in church on Mothering Sunday to donate ten per cent of whatever they will have spent on a card, a gift and even a meal out to thank their mum, to the Mothers' Union.

Another organisation that supports families, particularly in stressful situations, and which it would be appropriate to support financially, is Care for the Family. Mothering Sunday is not a happy occasion in all families.

* * *

Easter garden competition

Date: Holy Week

Web links

www.barnabasinchurches.org./8065 (to download précis of Easter story to accompany competition entry form and publicity flier)
www.biblelands.org.uk
www.childrenssociety.org.uk

Introduction

Competitions are always popular, particularly with children, and often attract entries from a wider group of people than just the church family. An Easter garden competition helps to share the story of Easter while building relationships into the community.

Key Bible verse

In the place where Jesus had been nailed to a cross, there was a garden with a tomb that had never been used.
JOHN 19:41

Bible links

- Matthew 26—28
- Mark 14—16
- Luke 22—24
- John 18—20

Key focus

Sharing the Christian story; fundraising for charity; fun

Key group

Children; schools; local community; families

Activity ideas

Invite everyone to create an Easter garden on a plate.[15] Provide some simple instructions for competitors to follow, and use a china or thick paper plate no bigger than 30cm diameter as the base. The garden must show something of the Easter story in the Bible. (Provide a simple précis to hand out with the entry forms or publicity fliers. This can be downloaded from the Barnabas website.) Give information about where and when entries need to be delivered. Set the date so that there is time for viewing and to allow time for judging. This needs to be at least two hours beforehand, but could equally be the previous day. Also, it could be part of a service if the display will be in the church

Offer three age-group classes. These might be under 8 years, 9–16, and 17 and over (if adults are to be included). Alternatively, have separate classes for under 6, 7–9, and 10–12. The decision will depend on whether the competition will be focused on a primary school, a uniformed organisation or across the whole community.

Charge a small entry fee, but make it clear that it is a donation to charity (not the church, but for Bible*Lands* or The Children's Society or another charity that the church supports). The prize(s) could be books about the Easter story, and it may be possible to provide a small Christian book for every entrant. Make sure that the winning entries clearly illustrate something of the Easter story as well as being of artistic merit.

— Prayer —

Father God, from the garden of Eden to the garden of resurrection you have shown us your love. May we learn more of your love as we create our Easter gardens.

Developing the theme

The most effective way to reach children and their families is to run the competition through the local primary school. Produce a simple sheet of instructions for children, and a more detailed explanation on the reverse for adults. Take in a couple of examples to demonstrate the possibilities. Provide a fibre-moulded disposable plate for each child to use. Arrange for all the entries to be displayed on tables in the school hall and invite someone who is not part of the local community to be part of the judging team and to present the prizes. Have place cards or rosettes to indicate the first, second and third place winners so that they can be easily identified when the pupils are invited to tour the display. Invite parents and friends to visit the display, too.

If you are invited to lead an assembly to link with the competition, an appropriate song to sing would be 'Were you there when they crucified my Lord?'

Developing the theme on a grand scale

If there are local people who like making artwork on a large scale, invite them to create scarecrow-style figures of the characters in the Easter story to display in gardens around the parish. You will need to depict scenes from the story, including the two disciples meeting the man who owns the donkey, Jesus riding on the donkey (with people waving palms), the scene of the last supper, Jesus being arrested, Jesus being tried, three crosses, the tomb with the stone rolled across the entrance and, finally, the empty tomb. This would be a massive community project, so it might be wise to start with

Jesus on the donkey, the cross and the empty tomb in the first year and then add more scenes each year.

Another approach would be to ask different groups, such as local schools, pre-schools, uniformed organisations, lunch clubs, care homes for the elderly and so on, to take on one scene each. Such a project needs at least one person with huge passion to make it happen.

* * *

Good Friday gathering

Date: Good Friday or another day in Holy Week

Introduction

The 'Seasonal activities' section of this book provides a script and series of activities for everyone to learn about all the events that surround the crucifixion and resurrection (see pages 37–42). Another way to help children and adults understand more of the Easter account is to offer a series of workshop activities. These could be offered in the hall while the main church is used for a more traditional three-hour observance.

Key Bible verse

Jesus began telling his disciples what would happen to him. He said, 'The nation's leaders, the chief priests, and the teachers of the Law of Moses will make the Son of Man suffer terribly. He will be rejected and killed, but three days later he will rise to life.'
MARK 8:31

Bible links

- Matthew 27—28
- Mark 15—16
- Luke 23—24
- John 19—20

Key focus

Sharing the Christian story; providing sacred space for reflection

Key group

Church family; schools

Activity ideas

Choose activities that can be organised simply, such as some of the following ideas.

Banner

Use a large A2 sheet of card to create a banner. Start with a large, simple outline of a cross drawn on the card. Talk about the sadness and despair the disciples must have felt to see Jesus being killed. Provide tissue paper in sombre colours, such as ochre, grey, black and dark brown. Invite people to tear off sections of tissue paper, about 4cm square, scrunch them up, dip them in PVA glue and then press them on to the cross outline. Once about half of the outline has been covered in this way, sit back to reflect on the work so far.

Talk about what happened next: Jesus' body was removed from the cross and laid in a tomb and, by Easter morning, it was gone because he had been brought back to life in a new way.

Now provide fresh supplies of tissue paper in joyful colours—these could be bright shades of blue and purple, shades of yellow and gold or rainbow tints—so that signs of new life blossom on the outline cross.

Bible study

Read the account of the burial of Jesus from John 19:38–42 in several different translations, including from a children's Bible. Discuss some of the following questions.

- Why was Joseph of Arimathea afraid of the Jewish authorities?
- What had changed for Nicodemus? He first visited Jesus by night, but here he is taking Jesus' body in broad daylight.
- Is it significant that Jesus was buried in a garden?
- It obviously mattered to the writers of the Gospels that the tomb was new. Is there any reason for this?

Count the crosses

Search the church building, if the event is taking place there, to count the number of crosses displayed (look at windows, architecture, pictures, signs, books and so on). Talk about why the church has so many crosses. Then draw a favourite one that has been found, or design one to share something of the Easter story.

Easter cards

Provide sheets of thin A4 card and felt-tipped pens and crayons. Invite everyone to make a card that shows something of the crucifixion as well as Easter Day. Give some examples, such as a stark cross on the front cover in black and white but with an explosion of colourful flowers inside; or people looking downcast on the front, but joyful inside.

The Easter story through cards

Provide a wide range of Easter greeting cards, including secular ones. Decide whether any of the cards should be omitted: for example, the group may decide to leave out a card that shows a baby rabbit. Discuss as a group the best sequence for the images to tell the story of Easter. Lay the cards out in the order that has been decided so that everyone can see.

Edible Easter gardens

Use a crispbread as the base and place it on a paper plate. Spread with soft cheese. Mix spoonfuls of soft cheese with crushed savoury biscuits and make a mound at one end of the crispbread to be the tomb. Add three mini savoury sticks to the mound to represent the three crosses. Use a mini rice cake to close and open the tomb and lay a trail of linseed or poppy seeds to create a path to the tomb. Sprinkle some mixed herbs across the rest of the base to represent grass. Add some flower-shaped sweets (or flower icing decorations).

Talk about why each element of the garden is included as people make their gardens.

Looking at art

Display several different reproductions of paintings of the crucifixion. These can be displayed on PowerPoint or printed out.[16] Discuss the different ways in which the crucifixion has been portrayed. (Knowledge of art history is not required: the main thing is to look at the emotions and different styles depicted.)

Musical reflection

Listen to a section of Handel's *Messiah*, such as the aria 'All we like sheep' (No. 26), or a piece from Bach's *St Matthew Passion*, such as 'O sacred head, sore wounded' (No. 54). Next, choose a traditional hymn about Good Friday, such as 'When I survey the wondrous cross', and, finally, listen to a more modern worship song, such as 'How deep the Father's love for us'. Discuss how effective they are, which piece people prefer and why.

Prayer encounter

Talk about how Jesus used his hands in life (to bless, to heal, to eat, to give thanks, to break bread) and as he died. Invite everyone to think about how they use their hands. Acknowledge that sometimes hands are used in anger and to hurt, as well as to look after others and be kind.

Encourage people to draw around one of their hands and to cut out the hand shape. Smaller children may need help with this. As they work, ask people to think about how they use their hands and to pray about good ways to use them. Finally, invite them to lay their hand shapes at the foot of a large cross. Some churches may have a large wooden cross to which the hand shapes can be fastened.

Song

Learn a song or hymn that tells some part of the Holy Week and Easter story. Possible choices include 'Come and see' and 'See, what a morning, gloriously bright'.

— Prayer —

God of all creation, we pause today to think about Jesus being killed on the cross. Guide our thoughts, open our hearts and refocus our lives. Amen

Developing the theme

Offer similar workshops to schools that wish to visit the church to experience Easter, or invite local uniformed organisations, such as cubs or guides, to take part.

* * *

All-age vigil

Date: Easter Eve

Introduction

Some churches organise a vigil on the Saturday evening to prepare to celebrate Easter the next day. This is an opportunity to provide an additional activity so that children and families can observe the occasion in a more informal way.

Key Bible verse

Here is the Lamb of God who takes away the sin of the world!
JOHN 1:29B

Bible links

- Psalm 85:2 (God forgives sin and takes away guilt)
- Isaiah 53:10 (God's servant suffered to take away sin from his people)

Key focus

Sharing the Christian story; providing sacred space for reflection

Key group

Church family; children

Activity ideas

The wall of sins

Invite everyone to name things that come between us and God, such as how we use our time, anger, sin or greed. Write each suggestion on to the side of a separate shoebox or large grocery box with a marker pen. Build a wall of the boxes as the ideas are suggested. Ask a couple of people to help keep the wall stable, as the more boxes are added, the more unstable it will become. It may be necessary to use cheap parcel tape to help keep the wall together as it grows.

Point out that the more sins there are—the more things that get in the way—the harder it becomes to see God. Explain that when Jesus died on the cross, he broke down the wall that people build up between themselves and God. Use a large cross to smash through and break down the wall from behind.

Darkness to light

Provide sugar, crêpe and tissue paper in black and white, chalks and crayons. Invite everyone to make a collage or draw a 'darkness to light' picture.

Through the tunnel

Stretch out a children's play tunnel.[17] Cover it with a blanket to make the tunnel darker. Place a desk lamp to shine brightly on to the exit at the far end.

Invite everyone to think about how dark the world is without the light of Jesus to brighten it.

Ask anyone who wants to remember their baptism, the journey from darkness to light, to crawl through the tunnel towards the light. Invite everyone who has already crawled through the tunnel to stand at the lit end to cheer as each new person emerges into the light.

— Prayer —

Holy God, you have the power to bring us from darkness to light. As we wait to celebrate the joy of Easter and the miracle of the resurrection, help us to share the light of Jesus with the world.

Developing the theme

Invite everyone to renew their baptismal promises as they prepare to celebrate Easter.

* * *

Christian Aid week

Date: second week of May

Web links

www.christianaid.org.uk
www.barnabasinchurches.org.uk/8065 (to download 'bear' script)

Introduction

The fundraising that takes place in Christian Aid week, and the related opportunities to campaign for better life chances for people across the world, provide a useful chance to make links with local children and families in the course of fundraising.

Key Bible verse

'When I was hungry, you gave me something to eat, and when I was thirsty, you gave me something to drink. When I was a stranger, you welcomed me.'
MATTHEW 25:35

Bible links

- Zechariah 7:10 (look after widows, orphans, foreigners and those in need)
- Matthew 25:35–40 (Jesus instructs us to feed the hungry and welcome strangers)

Key focus

Campaigning and social action; fundraising for charity

Key group

Children; schools

Activity ideas

Arrange to visit a local nursery, toddler group, pre-school or reception class to provide a simple explanation to the children of the meaning of Christian Aid week. The following story, by Nicholas Orme, is a good introduction for young children. If a pre-school wanted to hold a fundraising event, children could be asked to bring their own teddy bear along to hear the story and to bring, say, a 50p coin. After it has been told, create a display with all the props used in the story as well as some literature from Christian Aid.

You will need a big bear and a small bear, plus some extra bears to be pushed aside; two towels for beds; drinks cans; plastic bottles; a screw of paper; a big box; a lemonade bottle; sticky tack; a Christian Aid collecting box or envelope; a maraca or rainstick for sound effect.

A bear story for Christian Aid week

This is Big Bear. She pushes people aside if they get in her way. *(Push the other bears aside.)*

This is Small Bear. He holds the door open for people. *(Mime this.)* Big Bear goes through, and doesn't say thank you.

Big Bear throws litter all over the place. Paper, tins AND bottles. *(Do this with the props.)*

Small Bear picks up the litter and puts it in the recycling box. *(Mime this.)*

Big Bear never listens. As soon as someone starts talking, she starts talking even louder! *(Mime this.)*

Small Bear listens. He sits very quietly and listens for the Holy Spirit. *(Soft maraca or rainstick noise.)*

Big Bear likes lemonade, but she will NOT let anyone else have any. *(Mime this.)*

Small Bear likes Christian Aid. The Holy Spirit told him about poor people in other countries. So he puts some money into an envelope and gives the envelope to Christian Aid to help them. *(Mime this.)*

Big Bear is going to bed. *(Lay out a rumpled towel.)* She feels cross and thinks, 'The garden is full of litter. The kitchen is a mess. So is my bed. It hasn't been made properly. It feels sticky. Yuk! There's some chewing gum in it.' Big Bear hasn't done anything interesting or helpful all day.

Small Bear is going to bed. *(Lay out a neatly folded towel.)* He feels happy and thinks, 'I listened to the Holy Spirit and thought about people in need. I did something helpful today. I sent them some help through Christian Aid.' Small Bear turns out the light and goes to sleep.

Big Bear is still trying to get rid of the chewing gum. Oh dear!

— Prayer —

Father of all, thank you that you have provided enough for everyone. Help us to share the riches we have with people who do not have anywhere near enough.

Developing the theme

Hold a teddy bears' afternoon in church, or in a school or library. Place picnic rugs on the floor and provide plenty of teddy bears for children to play with. Offer a simple craft, such as decorating a teddy bear shape cut from thin card with a face and paws. (Crayons work well, but circles of fur fabric for the paw pads would be fun to glue on.) Tell the story above and then serve teddy bear-shaped biscuits and juice. Either charge 50p admission for each child or invite donations to Christian Aid towards the end of the event (but make this clear beforehand in the publicity). Aim to keep the event to 45 minutes so that children will not be overwhelmed by activity.

* * *

Day of prayer

Date: Ascension, or at any other time of the year

Web links

www.24-7prayer.com
www.orisonschools.org.uk

Introduction

Starting from the idea that Jesus was taken up into heaven, Ascension is a good day to open the church for a day of prayer—when prayers will be offered up to heaven. A Sunday may be a better day to hold a day of prayer with services forming part of the day's activities. Of course, a formal day of prayer can take place on any occasion, not just at Ascensiontide.

Key Bible verse

Always be joyful and never stop praying. Whatever happens, keep thanking God because of Jesus Christ. This is what God wants you to do.

1 THESSALONIANS 5:16–18

Bible links

- Isaiah 56:7 (God's house will be a house of prayer)
- Mark 12:42–44 (the widow's offering of two coins)

Key focus

Providing sacred space for reflection

Key group

Church family; schools; local community; families

Activity ideas

Arrange for the church to be open for at least twelve continuous hours on one day. Organise a rota of people to take an hour or half-hour slot during the day to pray, so that prayer will be offered continuously through the event. This will also ensure that the church is being looked after. It is advisable for at least two people to be on duty at any one time. Invite people from the local community also to sign up for a prayer slot, so that there may be several people in the church praying at the same time.

Good publicity will be needed for this event. Deliver an invitation for prayer requests to every house in the area. Explain when the church will be open, what people will be able to do in the church, and how they can take part by submitting a prayer request. Provide a tear-off slip on the invitation for people to use to submit a written prayer.

Contact the local press with an invitation for prayer requests. Provide a contact telephone number or email address if possible, so that people can get in touch. Explain that prayer requests can also be left at the church or in a collecting box located in a pub, shop, school or surgery. Invite the local school(s) to submit their own prayers. They may wish to make a visual display of their prayers to put on view. This invitation could be extended to the pre-school, to uniformed groups and to care homes.

Start the event with a set liturgy for morning, or another formal act of worship. End the day with an evening liturgy, or with some other way to gather up all the prayers of the day to offer them to God. For example, a traditional prayer meeting may be planned to close the proceedings. Some churches will decide to offer a lunch-time Communion service or a time of formally led prayer during the day.

Provide a range of prayer activities. Try some of the prayer pilgrimage ideas on pages 44–46 to make use of features in the building. At the same time, many of the prayer ideas in this book can be used or adapted (see index on page 222). Other ideas may include the following.

- Provide a collection box for prayers, along with paper and pens, for people to write and submit private prayers. Provide an explanation that all the prayers in the box will be offered to God at the closing act of worship without being opened.
- Make a prayer board to which people can add their own prayers for others to pray with them. Make it clear that only first names or initials should be used, to ensure privacy.

- Provide a large sheet of plain card, headed 'Portrait Corner', stuck to a wall or display board, with pens. Invite everyone to draw a portrait of themselves on the card, and then to pray for someone else already drawn on the card.
- Set out a basket of copper coins. Display the Bible verses about the widow's offering and invite people to take two coins out of the basket. Ask them to hold the coins and pray about how they spend their money. Invite them, at the end of their prayer, to return one coin to the basket as an act of intention, and suggest they put the other coin into their pocket to remind them of their prayer.
- Provide a selection of Bible verses printed on to small cards. Obvious choices would be Psalm 46:10, John 3:16 and 1 John 4:7, but local circumstances may suggest others. Invite people to browse through the cards until they feel drawn to a particular verse. Suggest they sit quietly to reflect on the words for a few minutes. Explain that they are welcome to take their chosen card home to continue their prayer.

Provide simple refreshments for visitors to enjoy. Provide the materials to make tea, fruit tea and coffee, and hot water in a flask. Make sure the supplies are replenished during the day.

One parish in Devon organised a day of prayer and was surprised by the level of response. In particular, one elderly couple came into the church for the first time in years. They sat together quietly for a while and enjoyed a cup of tea. The wife died, unexpectedly, just a few days later, and the husband subsequently joined the congregation.

— Prayer —

Lord, teach us to pray. (Luke 11:1)

Developing the theme

If the event has gone well, consider extending the opening hours next time. Even if 24 hours is too difficult to arrange because of lack of people or because the area is not safe, it may be possible for the building to be open from 6am to 9 or 10pm.

Invite young people who are part of the church family to help develop the prayer activities and to provide the closing act of worship. Uniformed groups can be asked to do this if there is no youth group.

If the event does not attract much interest the first time it is undertaken, try again a year later. Some activities need gentle and continuing encouragement to come to full flowering.

* * *

Windmill fiesta

Date: Pentecost

Web link

www.biblesociety.org.uk

Introduction

The account of the day of Pentecost starts with the sound of a strong wind filling the house where the Lord's followers were gathered. This idea uses 'wind' as the theme for an activity session. Most references to wind in the Old Testament refer to a frightening and destructive force, although it is a positive wind that breathes life back into the dry bones seen by the prophet Ezekiel. For Jesus to calm the wind in the storm, and then to talk about the Holy Spirit like a wind, would have seemed strange to the disciples.

Key Bible verse

Only God's Spirit gives new life. The Spirit is like the wind that blows wherever it wants to. You can hear the wind, but you don't know where it comes from or where it is going.

JOHN 3:8

Bible links

- Psalm 119:105 (God's word is a lamp that gives light)
- Ezekiel 37:1–14 (the valley of dry bones)
- Matthew 8:23–27 (Jesus calms a storm)
- Acts 2:1–12 (the coming of the Holy Spirit)

Key focus

Sharing the Christian story; fundraising for charity; fun

Key group

Church family; children; schools

Activity ideas

Invite everyone to a windmill fiesta activity session. Welcome everyone by setting up a bubble-blowing machine at the entrance or ask a family to stand there blowing bubbles from small pots.

As everyone gathers, invite them to join in a game of 'When the wind blows', which is a variation on 'Simon says' (see page 206). Actions that can follow the command 'When the wind blows' include: smile; windmill round your arms; be happy; stand still and listen; wave at someone; dance on the spot. Actions to announce without the command, and thus not to be done, include: scowl; groan; make a nasty face; stamp feet; be cross.

After the game, from a children's Bible read the account of the Holy Spirit coming like a mighty wind to the early believers. This sets the scene for the session's activities.

Provide three or four activity stations for people to visit in their own time, from the following suggestions.

- Decorate a blank children's windmill with pictures to show something of God's power.[18]
- Make a single large-scale children's windmill from scratch[19] and invite everyone to add a Bible verse or prayer on one of the four wings.
- Create a large collage of a real windmill. Invite everyone to add on to the sails the names of people who particularly need God's strength.
- Lay out a miniature obstacle course on a trestle-style table. Use small boxes and containers to create the obstacles. It would be fun if one of the obstacles looked like a windmill. Create a boundary wall around the table using corrugated or thick card and parcel tape to stick it on (this will ensure that the ball does not roll off). Provide a new drinking straw for each person and challenge them to blow a ping-pong ball around the obstacle course. To make it competitive, if desired, time each contestant.
- Provide long lengths of thin lining fabric or organza. Experiment with sending gusts of air from one end of the fabric to the other. With people holding the fabric at either end, practise wafting it up into the air and watch as it slowly descends. This could also be done with a play parachute, provided the fabric is not too thick (a real parachute is thinner and works better).
- Display several Bibles in different versions, with Acts 2:1–12 clearly marked. Also supply children's storybooks that explain about the Holy Spirit[20] as well as writing and drawing materials. Provide some chairs or beanbags so that those who want to read, write or draw may do so.

As the session draws to a close, sing (or learn) the song 'Jesus, be the centre' and encourage everyone to make movements to the words as they sing. Some groups will find it easier to take part with movements if someone demonstrates possible actions for the words first.

Offer any of the prayers that have been recorded on to the large windmill and invite people to take turns to walk under the lengths of fabric (or parachute) as they are wafted high into the air, to be refreshed by the power of the Holy Spirit as everyone else prays for them.

Ask everyone when they go home to display their windmill in their garden, on a balcony or at a window as a sign of the Holy Spirit at work in the neighbourhood.

— Prayer —

Loving God, thank you for sending your Holy Spirit to guide, comfort and inspire us. Give us the strength to share our love for you with other people. Amen

Developing the theme

On the day of Pentecost, the account in Acts emphasises that everyone heard the Lord's followers speaking in their own language. Pentecost is a good occasion to welcome a speaker from Bible Society to talk about the continuing need for the Bible to be translated into other languages. Invite donations to support translation work for one particular language that interests the church family.

* * *

Trinity party

Date: the Sunday after Pentecost

Introduction

The theology of the doctrine of the Trinity (that we have one God who is Father, Son and Holy Spirit) is hard for many of us to understand. A meal that has everything in threes is a fun way to celebrate the feast of Trinity, even if it does not explain the doctrine.

Key Bible verse

About that time Jesus came from Nazareth in Galilee, and John baptised him in the River Jordan. As soon as Jesus came out of the water, he saw the sky open and the Holy Spirit coming down to him like a dove. A voice from heaven said, 'You are my own dear Son, and I am pleased with you.'
MARK 1:9–11

Bible links

- Isaiah 40:28–29, 31 (our eternal God is the Creator and source of wisdom and strength)
- Matthew 28:19 (Jesus instructs his disciples to baptise people in the name of the Father, Son and Holy Spirit)

Key focus

Sharing the Christian story; fun

Key group

Church family

Activity ideas

Organise a 'Trinity' meal to follow a service or a children's activity. Ideas for the menu may include the following items.

- Pretzels (traditionally thought to represent the Trinity).
- Trinity burgers made with a roll, meat or veggie-burger, and one choice of onions or ketchup (explain why there can only be three elements).
- Trinity sandwiches made with bread, spread and filling.
- Trinity salads made from anything with three ingredients.
- Trinity jacket potatoes with one main filling and another topping.
- Trinity trifle with three distinct layers of sponge, custard and cream, or three similar layers according to local taste.
- Trinity fruit salad made from three fruits such as oranges, strawberries and apple.
- Trinity bananas (point out that bananas have three sides as well as three letter 'a's).
- Trinity sundaes made with a scoop of two different flavours of ice cream topped with sauce or a chocolate flake.
- Trinity sponge cake with jam in the middle and water icing on the top.

Cover the tables with banqueting roll,[21] provide crayons and felt-tipped pens in only three colours, and invite everyone to decorate the table coverings with three-sided doodles. Make sure that serviettes are provided, folded into triangles.

Provide some simple activities involving the number three, so that quick eaters have something to do while others finish their meal, such as the following ideas.

- Wander round the room in threes and see how many triangle shapes or sets of three can be seen.
- Try three-legged walking. Challenge older children to try four-legged walking with three people having their legs tied together.

- Provide a game of Triominos for older children to play.
- Cut triangles out of thin card in various sizes so that younger children can create people, robots and flowers.

— Prayer —

This traditional prayer from the 13th century, by St Richard of Chichester, has three distinct parts:

O most merciful Redeemer, Friend, and Brother,
May I know thee more clearly,
Love thee more dearly,
And follow thee more nearly:
For ever and ever.

Developing the theme

Challenge people to find a church that is dedicated to the Holy Trinity and to send the church greetings for its special day. Look on the internet via a search engine to locate the churches. Some churches will have their own website with a 'contact us' option so that a greeting email can be sent. For others, send a postcard.

Ask a group of young people to research the list of churches with contact details, and then invite church members to take responsibility for contacting an individual 'Trinity' church.

Mission ideas for Summer (June, July and August)

During the summer months, routines and schedules can become more relaxed for families. This may mean that they are more open to trying new activities or taking part in one-off events. Put simply, they may have a little time to spare. Indeed, for some families, the school holidays may pose a problem because there is too much time and not enough activity or money.

Churches can use the longer evenings, and the opportunities offered by the school holidays, to provide activities for children and all the family. There are fewer major festivals in the Christian calendar across the summer, although St James' Day is a chance to undertake a mini-pilgrimage, so the shape of the summer months is directed by community events.

Volunteers' week

Date: first seven days in June

Web link

www.volunteersweek.org.uk

Introduction

This national week celebrates the contribution of volunteers to British life. It provides an opportunity to encourage church members to donate some of their time out to the community. Nearly half the adult population of the United Kingdom volunteer in some capacity, giving an average of 1.9 hours per week, but many Christians donate their voluntary work to the Church.

Key Bible verses

You are like salt for everyone on earth.
MATTHEW 5:13A

You are like light for the whole world.
MATTHEW 5:14A

Key focus

Building community relationships; campaigning and social action

Key group

Church family

Activity ideas

Celebrate the involvement of church members in voluntary work by providing a large 'graffiti' sheet of paper, attached to a wall, or a large memo board on which everyone can record the voluntary work they do. Divide the paper into categories with headings such as charities; working with children and young people; community action; working with elderly people; working with people with special needs; overseas development; sports and so on. Add any other categories appropriate to the area. Make sure children are given the chance to add their contributions. During the intercessions at a service, invite the different groups of people identified above to stand, or raise their hand, for prayer. Some people may be prayed for more than once as they will be working in more than one category.

Invite people to contribute photos of the voluntary work they are involved in, to create a PowerPoint display or photo-montage to show in church. This could be used as the basis for prayers of intercession.

— Prayer —

Teach us, good Lord, to serve thee as thou deservest;
To give and not to count the cost;
To fight and not to heed the wounds;
To labour and not to ask for any reward, save that of knowing that we do thy will.
Through Jesus Christ our Lord.

ST IGNATIUS LOYOLA

Developing the theme

Ask a small group of people, including teenagers, to research which local organisations need voluntary support. This can be done by reading the local newspaper, consulting the local authority and volunteer agency, contacting the local media with a request for information and listening carefully in general conversation over a few weeks.

Assemble some information about the various volunteer vacancies that have been discovered. Invite the church family to pray for people to come forward to undertake the work—and ask them to consider if they are being challenged to serve God in this way.

* * *

Father's Day

Date: third Sunday in June

Web links

www.whatdadsadd.co.uk
www.gingerbread.org.uk
www.fnf.org.uk
www.crusebereavementcare.org.uk

Introduction

Father's Day is well established in the calendar. It is a parallel event to Mothering Sunday, although it has no Christian tradition behind it. Churches can use all the publicity and advertising surrounding the secular event to lead into their own activity.

Key Bible verses

Respect your father and your mother.
EXODUS 20:12A

Pay attention to your father.
PROVERBS 23:22A

Make your father truly happy by living right and showing sound judgment.
PROVERBS 23:24

Key focus

Campaigning and social action; fundraising for charity; fun

Key group

Families

Activity ideas

In some communities, families will not have much money to spend on making Father's Day special. In this situation, the church can provide a fun event that celebrates the role of fathers and does not require the family to spend a great deal of money. Simple ideas include screening an appropriate movie in the church or a local hall and providing popcorn and drinks for free;[22] organising a barbecue at the church; arranging a prebooked group expedition to a skating rink, fun park or cinema (to qualify for a group discount); hiring a swimming pool for an hour to be used by all the boys and men in the congregation. All the events require parents and carers to attend with, and be responsible for, their own children.

NB: When talking about these events, make it clear that children are welcome to bring either their father or any special person who is like a dad to them.

The 'What Dads Add' resources, sponsored by the Mothers' Union, provide many ideas to encourage fathers to nurture their child's spiritual development. The credit card-sized 'Wow, I'm a Dad' cards that can be downloaded from the website (see web link above) are good to hand to all fathers attending a Father's Day event, along with a bar of Fairtrade chocolate or a can of soft drink.

It is important to remember that some people, both children and adults, do not enjoy a positive relationship with their father. Others will not be able to spend time with their dad because he is working or because he is no longer part of the family. Ensure that any planned activities make it clear that everyone will be welcome, whether they can bring their dad along or not. If appropriate, display literature from support groups such as Families Need Fathers, One Parent Families, Gingerbread and Cruse bereavement care (see web link above). Churches may also wish to publicise or support the work of their local Child Contact Centre, where children of separated families can spend time with one or both parents.[23]

— Prayer —

Loving God, Jesus taught us to call you 'Father'. We pray for new dads, experienced dads, unhappy dads, absent dads, single dads, poorly dads, tired dads, confident dads, anxious dads and happy dads everywhere. May they reflect some of your love to their own children.

Developing the theme

Father's Day provides an opportunity to think about children whose fathers are in prison. Storybook Dads has a linked scheme, Storybook Soldiers, for members of the armed forces on active service to record a bedtime story CD for their children to listen to. Raise money at a Father's Day event to support the work of Storybook Dads.[24]

For churches that have few young families or no children, supporting charities that work with the children of service personnel, children with parents in prison, and children in difficult family situations, is a valuable way to work with children in the broader sense.

* * *

Midsummer's Day

Date: 24 June

Web links

Local community websites

Introduction

Many communities, rural and urban, hold parades to launch festivals or other celebrations of summer. Too often, churches are conspicuous by their absence from these events. This implies that church people do not have fun.

Key Bible verses

Our Lord, you bless those who join in the festival and walk in the brightness of your presence.

PSALM 89:15

Celebrate your festivals.

NAHUM 1:15B

Key focus

Sharing the Christian story; building community relationships; fundraising for charity; fun

Key group

Local community; families

Activity ideas

Create a 'walking entry' or a decorated float to take part in a community parade. If the main parade has an overall theme, follow that. For example, one town's festival and parade had an overall theme of 'Venice'. This would have enabled a church to join the parade with an entry based on the life of a well-known Italian saint, such as St Francis. An apt walking entry might have included an adult dressed as St Francis, accompanying children dressed as nativity figures (recalling that St Francis developed the first crib scene), and others dressed in animal costumes (to reflect his concern for the environment). The following year, the same town took the theme of 'shoes', which could have led churches to create an entry focused on 'holy ground' or 'pilgrimage'.

Organise one person to carry a large placard with details of the organising church(es) and accompanying adults to hand out leaflets (with details of any activities that take place for children and families at the church). As with any event, undertake a full risk assessment of the activity, inform the church's insurance company and make sure there are enough adults to supervise the children at all times. (See 'Putting it into practice', page 14, for a checklist to follow when planning an event.)

Gather a group of all ages together to plan the church's entry. Prayer and creative thinking will find an appropriate Christian contribution for any theme.

— Prayer —

Creator God, thank you for the fun of community celebrations. Help us to share your light as part of the festivities.

Developing the theme

Some of the bigger, illuminated carnivals require a huge level of investment to create floats worthy of the main procession, and it is important that entries are not substandard. To get involved with a local carnival, the church could offer a team of adults and older teenagers to carry some of the many collection buckets used to fundraise for the event's nominated charity. Alternatively, encourage church members to join in with other groups submitting entries.

* * *

St Peter's Day progress and picnic

Date: 29 June

Web link

www.barnabasinchurches/8065 (to download script)

Introduction

The life of St Peter provides exciting material for an activity session or whole day for children or all ages together. There is sufficient material for a whole day of activity, though it would work just as well to select a few of the ideas to use for a shorter session.

The principles demonstrated below can be adapted to create varied activities to 'walk through' any saint's day or church festival. Celebrating the patronal festival of a church is a good reason to invite people from the local community to share the fun.

Key Bible verses

Jesus saw two brothers. One was Simon, also known as Peter, and the other was Andrew. They were fishermen... Jesus said to them, 'Come with me! I will teach you how to bring in people instead of fish.' At once the two brothers dropped their nets and went with him.

MATTHEW 4:18–20

Bible links

- Matthew 14:22–32 (Jesus, and then Peter, walks on the water)
- Matthew 16:16 (Peter names Jesus as the Messiah)
- Matthew 16:19 (Jesus gives Peter the keys of the kingdom of heaven)
- Matthew 17:1–9 (the transfiguration)
- John 13:1–11 (Jesus washes the disciples' feet)
- Matthew 26:36–42 (Jesus prays in Gethsemane)
- Luke 22:54–62 (Peter denies that he knows Jesus)
- John 20:3–7 (Peter sees that Jesus' tomb is empty)
- John 21:1–19 (Peter meets Jesus again at Lake Tiberias)
- Acts 2:1–42 (Peter is filled with power by the Holy Spirit)

Key focus

Sharing the Christian story; fun

Key group

Church family; children; schools; local community; families

Activity ideas

You will need a narrator or storyteller with a copy of the script, and words written large to form the timeline of Peter's life as follows.

- Chosen
- Walking on water
- The Messiah
- Transfiguration

- Passover meal
- Garden of Gethsemane
- Crucifixion
- Resurrection
- Lake Tiberias
- Pentecost
- Chains
- Letters

The suggested activities follow the sequence of Peter's life. Choose as many as are practicable for the time or space available, but try to keep the order so that those taking part can follow the narrative of Peter's life. This will also enable participants to observe how Peter's faith changed and grew.

Appoint one person to be the narrator who will use the given script or include their own telling of each part of the story to provide a link into each different activity. A second person could give the instructions for the different activities. If you are working indoors, create a 'timeline' of the different events in Peter's life being marked during the session, using the key words.

Provide a quiet, reflective space in one corner of the room with comfortable chairs or beanbags, and artefacts that illustrate different aspects of Peter's life—such as a model fishing boat, a towel and small bowl of water, a small loaf of bread, chains, and a picture of Lake Galilee (which was also known as Lake Tiberias). A supply of paper-chain links for people to make up into longer chains would also work well. Provide some storybooks that tell the story of Peter, as well as copies of the Bible with some references to Peter marked so that anyone choosing to sit out of the activities can still share in the learning that is going on.

Gathering: Jesus chooses Peter

You will need a paper or card person shape for each individual attending (this could already have printed on it, 'Jesus chose Peter to be his disciple and Jesus chooses... [space for people to insert their own name] to follow him'); pens; fishing rod or net (or garden netting if necessary); sticky labels as name badges if required.

As everyone registers, invite them to write their name on to a person outline. The outlines can then be attached to the edge of a fishing net or on to the handle of a fishing rod. If the group do not know each other well, make sure everyone also has a name badge.

Game

Play a version of 'Simon says'. When the leader calls, 'Jesus says', everyone has to do that action. If the instruction is given without 'Jesus says' at the beginning, no one must do it. The 'Jesus says' actions could include 'smile'; 'rest' (with everyone sitting down); 'follow me' (walking behind the leader); 'pick up your cross' (mime putting something on their shoulder); 'praise God' (wave hands in the air); 'pray' (hands together) and so on. The instructions that are not to be done could include 'growl'; 'stand on one leg'; 'jump on the spot' and so on.

Narrator: Peter and his friends started to live alongside Jesus. Peter listened to Jesus telling stories and teaching people. He watched him healing those who were unwell and performing miracles. Peter must have been really puzzled about what was happening. Then, one night, after Jesus had managed to feed 5000 people from just five loaves of bread and two fish, something quite scary happened. Jesus sent the disciples ahead of him in a boat to get to the other side of the lake. The water of the lake was quite rough because the wind was blowing strongly. In the middle of the night, Jesus came across the lake to the disciples, walking on the surface of the water. Now the disciples were scared because they thought they were looking at a ghost, but Jesus told them not to be afraid because it really was him. Then Peter got out of the boat to walk alongside Jesus. When Peter looked down at the water, he began to sink, but Jesus grabbed hold of him and helped him into the boat. In our next activity we are going to pretend that we are walking on the water beside Jesus—and trusting him to look after us.

Walking on water activity

You will need two double-spread sheets of newspaper (or A2 sheets of card) for each group.

Divide everyone into groups of four or five with a mix of ages in each group. Give each group two double-spread sheets of newspaper. Everyone starts by standing on one newssheet at the side of the room. Each group then spreads the next sheet out and helps each member to step on to it before gathering up the first sheet. They continue in this fashion across the room with everyone only standing on one sheet of newspaper at a time. If the event is taking place outside, use sheets of cardboard from packaging, as newspaper will disintegrate too quickly.

Song

'He's got the whole world in his hand' or 'The journey of life' would be good choices to sing at this point.

Narrator: Soon after this, Jesus asked his disciples, his special friends, who people thought he was. Peter answered, 'You are the Messiah, the Son of the Living God.'

Memory verse

You will need each word of the memory verse written on to a separate A4 sheet of paper, or on a PowerPoint display, as follows: Simon Peter spoke up, 'You are the Messiah, the Son of the living God' (Matthew 16:16).

A way to learn this verse is to display all the words and then to chant them together at least three times. Next, remove the words 'Messiah', 'Son' and 'God' before chanting it again. Then remove 'Peter', 'you' and 'living' and chant it once more. Finally, hide all the words and get everyone to repeat again.

Another way to do this is to learn to sign it in British Sign Language, if someone in the group can demonstrate it clearly.

Narrator: Jesus was pleased that Peter described him as the Messiah because he thought it showed that God was really speaking to Peter. So Jesus said to Peter, 'I will give you the keys to the kingdom of heaven, and God in heaven will allow whatever you allow on earth.'

Keys of heaven craft activity

You will need key shapes, preprinted stickers and felt-tipped pens.

Provide everyone with a key shape, about 10cm long, cut out of card. It is also possible to order wooden keys.[25] One side could have a sticker with the words of the memory verse printed on it. Everyone then decorates the other side of the key with something that will help them to think about Jesus being the Messiah, God's chosen one.

Narrator: A short while afterwards, Jesus took Peter, James and John with him to the top of a high mountain.

Transfiguration craft activity

Follow the instructions for creating an edible mountain of the transfiguration (page 198). If everyone works in small groups, the account of the transfiguration can be told by the group leader at the same time as the instructions for creating the edible treat are given.

Alternatively, lead an imagination activity. Invite everyone to sit or lie on the floor with their eyes closed and encourage them to see what pictures come into their mind as they listen to an account of the transfiguration (Matthew 17:1–9) taken from a modern translation. Pause briefly as the reading is finished and then, as everyone keeps their eyes closed, ask if anyone wants to share what picture they have seen in their mind.

Narrator: Peter travelled all around Palestine with Jesus and the other disciples for three years.

Active game

Play 'follow-my-leader' with everyone following instructions to mime, such as climbing high mountains, rowing across the lake, sitting to rest, sleeping, walking and so on. Play this as a series of movements that follow each other around the space or, alternatively, after demonstrating the actions, call them out so that everyone has to do the action on the spot.

Narrator: Finally, Jesus led Peter and the other disciples to Jerusalem. They shared the Passover meal together, but before they ate Jesus washed his disciples' feet.

Foot-washing activity

You will need buckets or bowls of water and some towels.

Invite everyone who wants to, to wash someone else's feet. Remember that some people will feel uncomfortable with this activity so do not make it compulsory! Equally, ensure that children have the opportunity to wash the feet of adults, rather than it being something they have to have done to them. Some churches may choose to celebrate the Eucharist at this juncture.

Refreshments

Depending on the timing of your event, pause here to share lunch, which could simply be to eat packed lunches, or to share drinks and biscuits.

Narrator: After the disciples had shared the Passover meal, Jesus took them to the garden of Gethsemane so they could pray.

Prayer activity

You will need one sheet of thick A4 green paper or thin card per person; pens or pencils; several thick paper plates; glue.

Give everyone a sheet of green paper to represent the garden. Invite everyone to draw or write the prayers that they would like to share with Jesus in Gethsemane. Younger children will need parents or leaders to help them with this activity. Completed prayer sheets should then be rolled diagonally to make trumpet shapes. Glue several of these around the edge of thick paper plates to make flower shapes. Display the flower shapes on the wall or lay them around the fishing rod or net of the gathering activity.

Game

Remind everyone that Peter and the other disciples fell asleep while Jesus was praying. Then play 'Sleeping disciples', in which everyone has to pretend to be asleep without moving at all (see page 206).

Narrator: Jesus was arrested and taken to the house of the high priest. Peter followed behind to see what would happen to Jesus. As he watched, he was challenged three times about being a follower of Jesus. Each time he denied it. Then a cock crowed and Peter remembered that Jesus had predicted that he would say he didn't know him.

Game

Play a version of 'Grandma's footsteps' with everyone creeping up behind the accuser. When the accuser spins round to challenge someone with being a follower of Jesus, everyone has to run back to the beginning. When one person manages to creep up to the accuser without being caught, they tap them on the shoulder and take a turn of being the accuser.

Narrator: Jesus was killed on a cross on a Friday, and his body was placed in a tomb. Early on the Sunday morning, Peter went to the tomb with another disciple, John. Peter went into the tomb because the stone that had sealed it had been rolled away. He saw the linen clothes, in which Jesus had been wrapped, lying there. Suddenly Peter and John believed that Jesus had come back to life.

Prayer activity

You will need a space to represent the tomb. This could be a 'pop-up' garden tent, suitably covered with stone-coloured fabric, or there may be a cupboard that can be utilised to create a tomb to peer into. Arrange some white fabric to represent the folded grave-clothes, and a large lit candle if this can be done safely. If possible, find a large, rugged stone to place near the entrance. Put children's play sand into small polystyrene food trays so that individuals can draw patterns with their finger as they ponder, and provide tealight or votive candles to be lit from the main candle and displayed, possibly in a tray of sand (make sure that someone supervises this activity). Supply writing and drawing materials and offer a heap of small, rugged stones.

Explain that there is a choice of ways to reflect at the empty tomb, so everyone can make their own selection. Make it clear that there will be at least five minutes for people to pray and that they can try as many or as few activities as they wish. Remind them that the quiet corner has books to look at as well.

Narrator: The last time we read in the Bible about Jesus and Peter being together is at Lake Tiberias.

Acting out what came next

Take everyone back to the fishing net used for the gathering activity. Get everyone to stand in tight groups and pretend to fish on one side of a boat.

Narrator: Jesus appeared on the beach while Peter and his friends were fishing... unsuccessfully. Jesus told them to throw their net on the other side of the boat to catch something.

Invite everyone to pretend to heave up the net and cast it over to the other side.

Narrator: They caught so many fish—153 in total—that it was impossible to lift the net into the boat.

Pretend to haul the net in.

Narrator: Peter suddenly realised that it was Jesus on the beach. He gathered his coat around him and jumped into the water to swim ashore because he was so excited.

Invite everyone to mime putting on a coat, jumping out of the boat and then swimming across the room to the shore.

Narrator: The other disciples brought the net full of fish ashore, and Jesus took some of the fish and put it on to a small fire to cook. Then he took some bread and shared it with the disciples.

Pretend to eat fish and bread.

Narrator: Jesus asked Peter three times if he loved him. Then Jesus said to Peter one final time, 'Follow me!'

Refreshments

If the exploration of Peter's life is going to be concluded at this point, this could be the moment to share a picnic. It may be possible to provide fish and chips for everyone if there is a local shop or van.

Game

Play 'Follow my leader' again as a reminder that Jesus chooses everyone, and to lead the group into a space that can be the house where the disciples met on the day of Pentecost.

Narrator: On the day of Pentecost, Peter was in a house with the other people who believed that Jesus was the Messiah. Suddenly the house was filled with the sound of a strong wind blowing. As they looked at each other, there seemed to be tongues of fire spreading out and touching them. They were all filled with the Holy Spirit and they began to talk in other languages.

Bubbles activity

Provide everyone with a small pot of bubbles so that they can play and have fun. Let everyone share the excitement and playfulness.

Song

Sing 'O God of burning, cleansing flame' or 'The Spirit lives to set us free'.

Narrator: Pentecost was not the end of Peter's story. It was the beginning of a new and exciting chapter. He had been just a fisherman, but he found himself standing up to teach huge crowds of people about God, and he found himself explaining what he believed to the council of the Jewish elders. He found that the Holy Spirit sent him out into the world. He found himself in prison, bound up with chains. And he found himself set free from his chains, set free from prison by the power of the Holy Spirit. He also wrote letters to encourage people who wanted to follow Jesus. The letters were so important that they were kept and were included in the Bible.

Response and activity

You will need preprinted postcards (which can be produced on a computer), and pens and pencils.

Invite everyone to recall one thing they have enjoyed or learned during the session. It will help children, in particular, if you remind them of some of the activities, perhaps by pointing to the 'timeline' if you have created one. Ask everyone to share the 'best bit' of the event with someone else.

Remind everyone about the letters that Peter wrote. Then provide a postcard for everyone. On one side, have printed the following words, with space between them for people to write their response.

At the St Peter's progress and picnic I learnt...

The best bit was...

St Peter reminds me...

Provide a few minutes for people to complete these statements. On the other side of the postcard, ask them to write their name and address, before placing their cards by the fishing net. Finally, get everyone to stand around in a circle and say the Grace together.

The cards can be delivered to homes about a month later to remind everyone of their day together.

* * *

Linking with schools

Date: Second half of the summer term

Web links

Local schools websites

Introduction

After the late May Bank Holiday, schools become busy with sports days, residential visits and fundraising events.

Key Bible verses

He told our ancestors to teach their children, so that each new generation would know his Law and tell it to the next.
PSALM 78:5B–6

You are like salt for everyone on earth.
MATTHEW 5:13A

You are like light for the whole world.
MATTHEW 5:14A

Key focus

Campaigning and social action; building community relationships

Key group

Schools; church family; local community

Activity ideas

A good way to build links with a school is for a church to offer to organise refreshments for a sports day or similar event. If you do nothing else, make sure that members of the church family attend such events to support them and to help build community links. Barbecues, bazaars and fêtes can never have too many visitors.

Some schools find it difficult to get adults to help with residential visits. Active adults, who are willing to forego sleep, might find that an offer of assistance will be welcomed. The offer is more likely to be accepted if the adults have already started to build relationships with the school. For example, an adult who has attended assembly alongside a minister who is leading collective worship in a school will soon become known as a friendly supporter. Anyone who wishes to offer this help will have to be subject to full screening by the Independent Safeguarding Authority (ISA) through the school. Clearance through one's own church is not sufficient.

Many primary schools provide courses in life skills for pupils in Year 6 as they prepare to move on to secondary school. They may learn about fire safety or first aid, as well as ways to counter bullying. Some churches will have people with expertise in different areas of life skills who could offer to lead or contribute to some of the sessions. A church member could gain a qualification as a cycling instructor to teach cycling proficiency to children.[26]

A number of churches provide copies of *It's Your Move* (see page 210) for all the Year 6 pupils in the local school. This fun book provides helpful tips, activities and ideas to prepare pupils to move on to their secondary school. Some churches offer to lead a lesson or assembly based on the book to provide practical support at this anxious time of transition. Where churches are unable to work in partnership with the local school on this issue, these books can at least be given to children in the church family who are moving on to secondary education.

Church schools often attend a service to give thanks at the end of the year and to pray particularly for all those who are leaving. Churches could also extend an invitation to community schools. Many are delighted to have a specific reason to visit a local church to support the spiritual development of their pupils and to mark this important stage in their lives.

Further ideas that churches can use to work with their local school can be found in *Local Church, Local School* by Margaret Withers (Barnabas, 2010).

— Prayer —

Lord God, thank you for our local school(s). We pray that it (they) may be a welcoming community and a place of safety for all who work and study there.

Developing the theme

Younger children may also be at a point of transition, getting ready to move from nursery or pre-school to the reception class of the primary school. Provide copies of *Get Ready Go!* by Marjory Francis (see page 210) for all small children starting school in the area. It is easiest to do this through the local nursery or pre-school. If the church has already established good links with the nursery, it may be possible to organise a breakfast or tea-time session for these children and their parents or carers, to distribute the books and provide support.

Otherwise, give copies to the reception class teacher of the local school to distribute when the children visit, before they start. In this instance, offer to organise a simple tea party at the school on the day when children and parents are invited to visit.

Other churches, who have kept records of the babies they have baptised, dedicated or welcomed to a service of thanksgiving, can give a copy of *Get Ready Go!* to each child as they pass their fourth birthday. This would demonstrate the church's ongoing commitment to each child.

* * *

Holidays

Date: mid-July onwards

Web links

www.wastewatch.org.uk
www.scriptureunion.org.uk
www.cpas.org.uk
www.urbansaints.org
www.barnabasinchurches.org.uk

Introduction

Many churches wind down their activities from the middle of July until the new school year begins. This may be a good way to provide children's leaders with a well-earned break or it may happen because numbers attending are too low to sustain the usual programme. However, holidays can be 'holy' days, set apart for God from the usual activities.

Key Bible verses

By the seventh day God had finished his work, and so he rested.
GENESIS 2:2

'Remember that the Sabbath Day belongs to me.'
EXODUS 20:8

'People were not made for the good of the Sabbath. The Sabbath was made for the good of people.'
MARK 2:27

Key focus

Sharing the Christian story; building community relationships; campaigning and social action; fundraising for charity; fun

Key group

Church family; children; families

Activity ideas

Holiday clubs and activity sessions are good ways of reaching children and families. Details of organisations that publish Bible-based holiday club material can be found on page 210. If starting to run a full holiday club seems too daunting, even offering a single two-hour activity session will be of value to children and families.

Some churches decide to organise an all-age activity session to welcome children, parents, grandparents and anyone else interested. This makes it easier to provide activities for different groups of children and carers. In this instance, it is important to remind everyone that children remain the responsibility of the adult who has brought them, so that consent forms are not required.

One-off activity sessions can be an opportunity to try out the principles of Messy Church or to offer one of the sessions found in *Footsteps to the Feast* by Martyn Payne (see page 210). Other possibilities could be to arrange one of the following events.

- Healthy living day: With support from the local NHS trust or local authority, provide activities such as cookery, active games and fun.
- Reuse, reduce and recycle day: Include junk modelling, making planters to grow salad and herbs on a windowsill or balcony, and learning how to protect the environment.
- Arts, drama, reading or music session: Invite someone from the church family who has expertise, or pay for someone from the local authority or a specialist organisation to lead the day. In this way, the church is acting as a catalyst to enable children and families to learn something new and enjoy time together.
- Games session: Provide a range of traditional board and card games, such as Ludo, Cluedo, Snakes and Ladders, Game of Life, dominoes and draughts, and encourage everyone to have a go. Either start or end the session with a beetle drive (see page 204) to get everyone playing together.

— Prayer —

Lord of the Sabbath, help us to use our leisure time for your glory. As we rest in you, may we offer our talents in your service. Amen

Developing the theme

There are many organisations that provide holidays for children and families in particular need. All welcome financial support. Challenge the church family to fundraise to provide a holiday for less well-off families.

Christian organisations such as Scripture Union, Church Pastoral Aid Society and Urban Saints (formerly Crusaders) need volunteers to assist with the running of missions, holidays and house parties. The aim of these activities is to share the faith with the children and young people who attend. These organisations provide residential events to which churches can take groups of children, and this is a much easier option than trying to organise a residential holiday from scratch. They also welcome unaccompanied children.

A range of other charities that provide holidays or care breaks for disadvantaged families, or for those with seriously ill or disabled children, and which need assistance are listed on page 215.[27] Volunteers are often needed to help with catering, housekeeping and administration—not just leading children and young people's activities.

For some children, particularly if they are not going away, the summer holidays can seem dull and lonely. Resolve to send a postcard to every child in a church group at some point during the weeks when the group does not meet. Prepare sticky address labels before going on holiday so that sending cards does not take up too much time when away or, alternatively, buy the cards when away and write them after you return. The children will be thrilled to know that you are thinking of them. This is an easy and effective way to nurture relationships.

* * *

Out of the church

Date: Summer holidays

Web links

Local council websites

Introduction

People can be reluctant to come into a church building, however exciting the event or programme may be. It is often easier to get to know people out of the church and in space where they feel at home.

Key Bible verses

Very old people with walking sticks will once again sit around in Jerusalem, while boys and girls play in the streets.
ZECHARIAH 8:4–5

I praise you because of the wonderful way you created me.
PSALM 139:14

'Go out to the street corners and tell everyone you meet to come to the banquet.'
MATTHEW 22:9

Key focus

Building community relationships; campaigning and social action; fun

Key group

Children; families; local community

Activity ideas

Larger churches, or those working well with ecumenical partners, could host their own event in a local park or playing field. Written permission must be sought well in advance from the park authorities to stage such an event, and it is essential to provide adequate insurance cover. The event may take place for a single day or for several mornings or afternoons. Check that no other events are planned for the same dates, unless they will complement the church event, are willing to operate at the same time and will help to attract more people to attend.

Plenty of publicity before the event will be required to launch such a new venture and to make it clear that all activities will be free of charge. Provide an invitation for every child at the local school(s) to take home before the end of term and send a photo of a planning meeting for the event, with details of what will be on offer, to the local press. Ask the local paper to include details in their 'What's on' listings, and post information on websites that list events.[28] Contact the local radio station to get the event announced in their 'What's on' slot. Encourage church members to talk about the event to neighbours and friends.

The provision of a bouncy castle is always popular with children and will attract attention. Other activities to provide might include face-painting; simple crafts; toddler toy area; storytelling; 'Sumo wrestling' using hired padded suits; basketball, netball or football goal-scoring challenges; large-scale versions of Jenga, Connect 4, draughts, skittles and snakes-and-ladders; skipping ropes, hula hoops, spacehoppers; mobile skate park or a climbing wall.

Staging this type of event will incur expenditure. Those who are staffing the event should wear a uniform T-shirt or coloured sash for identification purposes.[29] Some of the games and activities suggested above can be borrowed from toy libraries, scrap stores or willing families, but other items will have to be bought or hired.

Some churches who stage such events also provide free home-made cakes and biscuits, along with juice and hot drinks as a present to their local community. Again, check with the park authorities about any restriction on providing refreshments. Put up gazebos to provide welcome shade on a hot day and a little shelter if it rains. Experience suggests that families still come along even if the weather is less than perfect. During the event, hand out leaflets with details of the church(es) organising the occasion, along with an invitation to attend a family service or something similar. If photographs are to be taken at the event, see the section on photographs on page 20. As with all similar events, parents and carers need to come with, and be responsible for, their own children.

— Prayer —

For sun and rain and happy days, thank you, Lord.
For fun to share and you to praise, thank you, Lord.
For things to do and friends to play, thank you, Lord.
For a wonderful world on this happy day, thank you, Lord.

Developing the theme

Alongside all the other activities, provide some simple prayer activities for everyone to do, such as supplying small sheets of paper, pens or pencils and a posting-box for people to post their written or drawn prayers. Ensure that the prayers are offered to God at a suitable service in church afterwards. Another idea might be to offer small, wrapped, chewy sweets and invite people to choose one and suck it as they thank God for something sweet and good they have experienced today. Alternatively, invite people to draw a small self-portrait on to a large sheet of card that is headed by the words, 'I praise you because of the wonderful way you created me' (Psalm 139:14).

* * *

Occasional offices

Date: Summer season

Web link

www.barnabasinchurches.org.uk/8065 (for downloads of sample activity sheets)

Introduction

Research suggests that up to 80 per cent of the population goes inside a church building every year. Some of those are attending regular worship or an occasional office, such as a baptism, wedding or funeral. Children often visit churches alongside adults for any of these purposes.

Key Bible verses

There is a time… for crying and laughing, weeping and dancing.
ECCLESIASTES 3:2, 4

When others are happy, be happy with them, and when they are sad, be sad.
ROMANS 12:15

Key focus

Sharing the Christian story; providing sacred space for reflection

Key group

Children; families; local community

Activity ideas

Churches can ensure a warm welcome to children and families who are attending an occasional office from another part of the country, or who are not regular attenders, by providing an activity sheet that links to the theme of the office and a choice of pencils and felt-tipped pens. A word search, a picture to colour, a maze and perhaps some 'Did you know?' facts about the occasion provide a way for children to begin to understand what is happening in the service. The story of Jesus' own baptism would make a good starting point for a baptism activity sheet, and the wedding at Cana for a wedding sheet. A sheet for use at funerals might be based on Psalm 23. Once such sheets have been prepared, they can be printed out again for use on future occasions. Provide clipboards to rest on to help children to fill in the sheets. (Sample activity sheets can be downloaded from the Barnabas website, www.barnabasinchurches.org.uk/8065.)

— Prayer —

Father of all, you have set times for weeping and times for dancing. Open our hearts to share the joy or sorrow of those who visit our church.

Developing the theme

Provide some Christian storybooks that link to the themes of baptism, wedding or funeral. Display them when required and make sure visiting families know that they can be borrowed. (Ideas for suitable books are listed on page 211.)

* * *

Welcoming tourists

Date: Summer holidays

Web links

www.divine-inspiration.org.uk
www.barnabasinchurches.org.uk/8065 (to download sample prayer stations sheet)

Introduction

Many families will look around church buildings when they are away on holiday or out for the day—particularly if it is wet. Others walk in off the street to find peace and a place to reflect, and yet others come as tourists to see the special features or historic elements of a particular church. This provides an opportunity to share something of the Christian faith and space for reflection, as well as the history of the building.

Key Bible verses

One day in your temple is better than a thousand anywhere else.
PSALM 84:10

Our God, here in your temple we think about your love.
PSALM 48:9

Key focus

Sharing the Christian story; providing sacred space for reflection

Key group

Families

Activity ideas

Adults visiting churches in search of history or church architecture will look for a guidebook or card to help them find features of particular interest. This can be a boring pastime for those accompanying them who do not share the same level of interest. It is straightforward to produce an activity sheet for children, to invite them to find tiny or amusing details inside the church, such as a mouse portrayed in a stained-glass window or the carving of a fox on a bench end.

However, this is at the level of a secular activity sheet, such as those produced by museums and stately homes, and misses the chance to draw children and any adults with them more into the life and purpose of the church. Ideas include putting on the activity sheet points of interest such as details of where to find a prayer board and inviting people to write or draw a prayer, offering an invitation to stand in (or look at, if it is out of bounds) the pulpit and imagine the priest telling people about the good news of Jesus, and inviting people to think about what good news they would give from the pulpit. Also, you could perhaps suggest that people sit very quietly and listen to all the different sounds they can hear outside the building, inside the church, and inside themselves. Finally, give information on where to find a display of some simple Bible storybooks, with plenty of illustrations, for children to read while they wait for the adults to look around the building.

The *Divine Inspiration* project based in the Diocese of Coventry has developed ideas for sharing church buildings with visitors.[30]

— Prayer —

Holy God, speak to us as we look around this church building. Call us to look at what you want to show us. May we feel that you are here with us now.

Developing the theme

If the church has many visitors to explore the building, it would be possible to develop some of the ideas for using parts of the building for prayer mentioned under St James' Day (see page 45), to provide activities for all ages.

* * *

Getting involved in summer fêtes and shows

Date: Summer season

Web link

www.playday.org.uk

Introduction

Many communities have outdoor events during the summer months, such as summer fêtes and shows, car boot sales, gardens open to the public, street markets, ploughing matches, garden competitions and so on. These are a good opportunity for the church to join in with the fun of the community.

National Playday, on the first Wednesday in August, is an initiative that encourages children and families to make time to play. Most Playday events are organised by a consortium of organisations that work with children and families, so churches are welcome to add their contribution.

Key Bible verse

You are precious to me, and so I will rebuild your nation. Once again you will dance for joy and play your tambourines.

JEREMIAH 31:4

Bible links

- Zechariah 8:4–5 (The streets will be safe)
- Matthew 22:9 (Take God's love outdoors)
- Mark 12:31 (Love others)

Key focus

Building community; campaigning and social action; fundraising for charity; fun

Key group

Children; local community

Activity ideas

If the event is taking place near the church, make sure the building is open and ready to receive visitors. Prop open the main door, have a board outside inviting people to come in, and arrange a rota of people to welcome them. Perhaps the church can help the main event by sharing facilities. For example, in one town, a tiny pocket park, tucked between blocks of flats, staged a World Food Party to help the many different nationalities living in the area to share their food heritage. The local Salvation Army temple opened its doors to provide lavatory facilities.

Get involved at an event by taking a pitch to ensure that the church has a presence. Provide pastimes for children (but do not take away income from commercial providers of bouncy castles, face-painting and so on). Have pots of bubbles to give away, just to spread fun (these can be obtained cheaply from pound shops or in bulk from the internet), and activity sheets on a theme linked to the event. Include some Bible teaching and details of any children's activities or appropriate services that the church is organising.

Organise an interactive prayer encounter for all ages, such as those given in the 'Out of the church' section on page 184.

One church created a baptism display, complete with a christening gown, photographs of recent baptisms, baptism candles and baptism cubes (see page 211) to remind the local community that they were welcome to consider baptism for their children or themselves. They gave away slices of cake and balloons to add to the fun. Three definite enquiries were received as a result.

— Prayer —

Lord Jesus, you taught us to love our neighbour as we love ourselves. Help us to get to know our neighbours so that we can learn to love them.

Developing the theme

One congregation takes the initiative to develop community relations by regularly inviting all the fundraising groups and clubs in the area to take a stall at a midsummer market held in the church building and yard. Trestle tables are laid across the pews to provide display space, and activities for children are organised in the churchyard. The church provides refreshments for sale but makes no charge to the other organisations that set up a stall.

* * *

Lammastide

Date: 1 August

Web link

www.thehungersite.com

Introduction

'Loaf-mass' has been marked since Anglo-Saxon times as the celebration of the first fruits of the new harvest, with a loaf of bread baked from the newly harvested wheat.

Key Bible verse

Jesus replied: I am the bread that gives life! No one who comes to me will ever be hungry. No one who has faith in me will ever be thirsty.
JOHN 6:35

Bible link

- John 6:11 (Jesus shares bread)

Key focus

Sharing the Christian story; fun

Key group

Children; local community; families

Activity ideas

Organise a bread-based activity session for children or for all ages together. Make bread dough together. Bake it during the session or, if there is no access to an oven, everyone can take their piece of dough, in a plastic food bag and with cooking instructions, to bake at home. Offer tastings of different kinds of breads from around the world. (Most supermarkets sell naan, pitta, brioche, tortilla, ciabatta, bagel, German rye, Jewish cholla, pretzels and Polish specialities.) Include some gluten-free examples so that anyone with gluten intolerance can take part.

Adapt the game 'Port and starboard' (see page 205) to play 'Basket of Bread', using 'wholemeal', 'white', 'rye' and 'seeded' to represent the four corners of the room and 'basket of bread' for the central gathering command. Alternatively, adapt the game 'Shapes' (see page 206) to play 'Bread shapes'. Use the phrase 'The baker says' in place of 'Simon says'.

- Roll: Curl up into a ball
- Breadstick: Stand tall
- Pizza: Make a round shape
- Loaf: Make a square shape
- Pretzel: Link hands

'Wrong' commands, to catch people out, should include food items not made of bread, such as:

- Crisps: Turn round on the spot
- Peanuts: Wave hands in the air
- Chips: Balance on one leg

Tell the story of Jesus feeding 5000 people with five small loaves of bread (John 6:1–13) or discuss the account of Jesus talking about being the bread of life (John 6:35). Offer a time of prayer and reflection. Ask everyone to sit quietly. Place a small baked roll in the centre. Invite everyone to give thanks for the food they will eat that day, and to pray for everyone in the world who will not have enough to eat. Hold a few moments of silence and then pass around the roll so that everyone can eat a small crumb.

— Prayer —

Jesus, you told us that you are the bread of life. Help us to share the food in the world so that none of God's children may be hungry.

Developing the theme

If it is not possible to organise a full activity session for a big group of people, invite some children to bake a small loaf for the Eucharist on the following Sunday.

Lammastide is a good occasion to encourage people to donate free food to those in need across the world by regularly visiting the website www.thehungersite.com and clicking to donate. Advertise the site in the parish magazine or weekly newssheet, or get it mentioned in the local newspaper.

* * *

The transfiguration

Date: 6 August

Web links

Webcam camera hire companies websites

Introduction

This is a day for memorable mountain-top experiences as the Christian year remembers how Jesus took three of his disciples to a high mountain for an amazing experience.

Key Bible verse

Six days later Jesus took Peter and the brothers James and John with him. They went up on a very high mountain where they could be alone. There in front of the disciples, Jesus was completely changed. His face was shining like the sun, and his clothes became white as light.

MATTHEW 17:1–2

Bible link

- Isaiah 42:11 (Celebrate in the mountains)

Key focus

Sharing the Christian story; fun

Key group

Church family; children

Activity ideas

It may be possible to open the church tower to the public as a special once-a-year event, if the insurance company will provide cover. Arrange activities inside the church for those waiting for their turn to ascend, and provide refreshments. If insurance cover cannot be obtained, set up a webcam to capture the view from the tower and project it on to a screen down in the church.

A fun activity to offer on this occasion would be to create an edible version of the transfiguration. Tell the story of the transfiguration or read it from a children's Bible. Remind everyone of the progression of the story as the different edible parts are assembled.

Make edible mountains by crushing digestive or ginger biscuits and then binding the crumbs together with soft cheese or thick honey. Older children can do the crushing (putting the biscuits into a plastic food bag and then tapping the bag with a rolling pin) and mixing for themselves, while younger ones can just model the shape with pre-prepared mix.

Put the mountain on to a small paper plate. Add a Smartie or Jelly Baby to represent Jesus and then cover it with a squeeze of white icing, from a tube of ready-to-use icing, to show the way Jesus' clothes became dazzling white. Next, use three Smarties or Jelly Babies of a single colour to represent Peter, James and John.

Then add two more sweets of a third colour to be Moses and Elijah. Finally sprinkle hundreds-and-thousands over the whole mountain as the cloud that covered everything (or use white icing or squirty cream). NB: if you use Jelly Babies, the mountain has to be a bit bigger!

— Prayer —

God of surprises, help us to be changed into the people you intend us to be, just as you showed the disciples Jesus' true glory.

Developing the theme

The edible transfiguration could also be made by children as part of their worship activities, or everyone could take part during refreshments at the end of a service that has focused on this particular reading. Use a visualiser to project what you are making, if you build up an edible model in a school assembly, as you speak.

* * *

Back to school

Date: late August

Web link

www.marysmeals.org

Introduction

For children, as August moves into September, their thoughts focus on returning to school. The shops will have been urging everyone to buy 'back to school' products since before the end of the summer term, but the final days of August are when children really look ahead. This is a good moment to hold an end-of-summer or back-to-school session to gather the children's group(s) together before the new term starts. Even if the church family only includes two or three school-age children, provide a small special event just for them. This is especially important for holding on to older children who may be looking for an opportunity to opt out of church. The beginning of the new school year, after the summer break, can offer such an opportunity to drop out.

Key Bible verse

I've commanded you to be strong and brave. Don't ever be afraid or discouraged! I am the Lord your God, and I will be there to help you wherever you go.
JOSHUA 1:9

Bible links

- Deuteronomy 31:6 (God is with you)
- Psalm 46:11 (God is powerful)
- Proverbs 3:5 (Trust the Lord)

Key focus

Providing sacred space for reflection; fundraising for charity; fun

Key group

Church family; children

Activity ideas

If the group has a wide age range, this is an occasion to invite only those children who are in Key Stage 2, or in Year 5 or above, to provide the chance for some more mature discussion (even if this means that the group is very small).

Invite everyone, including leaders, to bring photographs or souvenirs of anywhere they have been during the summer, and be ready to share some of your own experiences. Discuss together:

- What was fun?
- What was strange?
- What was the nicest food?
- Who did you meet?

Invite the children to bring a school folder to decorate, or give them one as a gift. (The cheapest source of ringbinder folders is any office supplies superstore. Alternatively, they can be ordered from the internet if there is no local outlet.) Provide a range of stickers, including Christian ones, for everyone to use to decorate the cover of the folders. Suggest some Bible verses for everyone to write on to address labels to stick inside the cover (use sticky-backed plastic to cover the inside cover to make the labels durable) and talk about their hopes and fears for the new school year. Then learn one of the suggested Bible verses and pray together. (Focus on relationships and fun, rather than formal teaching on this occasion.) Write the children's prayers (without names) into an exercise book, and then bring the book out later in the term to see how prayers have been answered. Play some games and sing favourite songs. Finally, share some chips and ketchup, pizza or other fun food.

Ask whoever will be leading the intercessions in church on the first Sunday after the beginning of term to include pupils, staff and governors, and the work of schools, pre-schools and colleges.

— Prayer —

O God, you are our mighty fortress. You are always ready to help in times of trouble. When we are scared, particularly at school, remind us that you are with us. Help us to value what we can learn at school when we remember that many children have few opportunities to go to school.

Developing the theme

The 'back to school' period is a good time to campaign for children who have few opportunities for schooling.

Mary's Meals is an international movement that sets up school feeding projects in communities where poverty and hunger prevent children from attending school (in Africa, Asia, Latin America and Eastern Europe). Some churches may wish to fundraise to feed some children for a year through Mary's Meals—currently less than £10 per child per year.

Others may wish to support the Backpack Project, whereby old schoolbags or backpacks are filled with school materials as well as soap, toothbrush and paste, flipflops and a spoon and despatched to children in need. Full details can be found on the Mary's Meals website.[31] This is a good opportunity to help children and adults alike to reflect on the huge variety of such materials available in this country, while other children have nothing. It also ensures that backpacks that have gone out of fashion can be reused rather than dumped. Good publicity will draw in people from the community to support such a campaign, organised locally.

Appendices

*

Generic games

Beetle drive

You will need paper and a pen for each player, and a dice for each group of four players.

People usually play sitting in fours around a small table, with the tables arranged in a circle around the room. Each player takes a turn to throw the dice. Each player must throw a six to make their first move, which is to draw a body for their beetle. In subsequent turns, they add on the other parts of their beetle as follows:

- Five is for the head, of which there is one.
- Four is for the tail, of which there is one.
- Three is for a leg, of which there are six (which means that a three must be thrown six different times to allow all the legs to be drawn).
- Two is for an antenna, of which there are two (two separate throws).
- One is for an eye, of which there are two (two separate throws).

The first player to add all the parts has to call out 'beetle' to halt play and is the winner of that round. Everyone adds up the score of their beetle (the body is 6, each antenna is 2 and so on; only the winner will have scored 35, the maximum possible) and records it on their game paper, which they keep with them. On each table, the winner, together with the person with the highest score after that, moves to the next table to the right. The person on each table with the lowest score moves down to the table on their left. The game starts again with everyone facing a blank sheet of paper and the need to throw a six. The overall winner will be the person who has the most completed beetles or the highest score at the end of the playing time. No skill is needed for this, so it is a good game for all ages to play together.

Fruit salad

Have four or five different items to represent the main elements of the story you are using or occasion you are marking. For example, at the Halloween Heroes party, use fire fighters, nurses, police officers, teachers and cleaners. Get everyone to sit in a circle, and then move round the group, giving each person in turn one of the five chosen items. When the item name is called out (for example, 'teachers'), people who have been given that item name have to change places with others who have the same item name (which will be those who have stood up to change places). Name the different items in turn and, from time to time, call out a name given to the whole group (in this instance, 'Halloween Heroes'), when everyone playing has to get up and change places.

Port and starboard

Each corner of the room represents one item, place or person in the theme you are illustrating, and the centre of the room represents a fifth. When the leader calls out the name of an item, everyone has to run to that space. This game can be played competitively so that the last person to arrive at the corner is 'out'. Alternatively, it can be played as a way to learn the key people, places or elements of a Bible story, with everyone moving around to the different spaces several times. For example, in the St Peter's Day progress, use 'mount of transfiguration', 'Gethsemane', 'Tiberias' and 'prison' as the four corners, plus 'Jerusalem' as the name for the centre of the room.

Simon says

The leader calls out actions that everyone has to do. Any moves should be made only if the leader first says 'Simon says' or another phrase of command. The most obvious command phrase could be 'Jesus says'. If the command phrase 'Simon says' is omitted, no one should move.

A variation on this game is 'Shapes'. At the beginning of the game, demonstrate a shape for each of the key words. The basic shape moves are as follows.

- Standing up tall with arms pointing to the sky (star)
- Rolling up into a ball on the floor (baby)
- Turning round on the spot (Joseph)
- Holding own hands together (Mary)
- Holding arms out to side, with elbows bent and hands pointing to floor (stable)
- Balance on one foot (angel)

Choose a word to label each action. For example, the words in brackets above indicate the words to call out to play a game based on the nativity story. In this way, when the leader calls out 'angel' everyone has to balance on one foot. When everyone has completed the shape, the leader calls out the next one.

Sleeping lions

Everyone lies on the floor and pretends to be asleep. Anyone who can be seen to move or heard to make any noise is eliminated. This is a good game to help everyone to calm down. It can be used to illustrate Bible stories, such as the disciples falling asleep in the garden of Gethsemane.

*

Suggested songs

All creatures of our God and king, *Hymns Old and New* (9)

As with gladness men of old, *Hymns Old and New* (41)

At the name of Jesus, *Hymns Old and New* (46)

Away in a manger

Come and see, *The Source* (70)

Come on and celebrate!, *Hymns Old and New* (95)

From the ends of the earth, *The Source* (115)

Give me oil in my lamp (Sing hosanna), *Kidsource* (66)

God's people aren't super-brave, super-heroes, *Kidsource* (86)

Have you heard the raindrops?, *Hymns Old and New* (202)

He's got the whole world in his hands, *Hymns Old and New* (206)

How deep the Father's love for us, *The Source* (185)

In the bleak midwinter, *Hymns Old and New* (248)

I want to see your baby boy, *Come and Praise* (117)

Jesus, be the centre, *The Source 2* (826)

King of kings, majesty, *The Source* (309)

Kum ba yah

Lift high the cross, *Hymns Old and New* (303)

Little donkey

Lord of the dance, *Hymns Old and New* (228)

Meekness and majesty, *Hymns Old and New* (335)

My God is so big, so strong and so mighty, *Kidsource* (255)

O, come, let us adore him, *Songs of Fellowship* (409)

O, God of burning cleansing flame, *Songs of Fellowship 2* (955)

O, Lord, all the world belongs to you, *Hymns Old and New* (378)

O, praise ye the Lord, *Hymns Old and New* (388)

Riding high and low, *Kidsource* (287)

See him lying on a bed of straw

See, what a morning, gloriously bright, *Songs of Fellowship 4* (331)

Silent night

Soon and very soon

Stay with me, *Hymns Old and New* (458)

Thank you for the cross, *The Source* (473)

There is singing in the desert, *Come and Praise* (26)

The first nowell, *Hymns Old and New* (477)

The journey of life, *Come and Praise* (45)

The Spirit lives to set us free, *Hymns Old and New* (494)

The virgin Mary had a baby boy, *Hymns Old and New* (496)

Unto us a boy is born

Were you there when they crucified my Lord?, *Hymns Old and New* (540)

We three kings

What child is this?, *Hymns Old and New* (542)

When I survey the wondrous cross, *Hymns Old and New* (549)

*

Recipe for Fairtrade cupcakes

100g butter or margarine
100g caster sugar
2 medium eggs
100g self-raising flour
1/4 teaspoon vanilla essence (optional)
1/4 teaspoon baking powder (optional)

Method

1. Beat the butter or margarine until soft, and then beat in sugar until soft again.
2. Add one egg at a time and beat the mixture well.
3. Gently fold in the flour.
4. Spoon enough mixture into a cupcake case to fill it two-thirds full.
5. Bake at 180°C/Gas Mark 4 for 10–15 minutes until golden in colour and springy to the touch.

To allow people to measure out the quantities for their own mix, use a dessertspoon as the basic measure:

2 level spoonfuls of softened butter or margarine
2 level spoonfuls of sugar
2 spoonfuls of beaten egg mixture
2 heaped spoonfuls of flour

Then proceed with the same method.

*

Bibliography

General resources

Messy Church, Lucy Moore (Barnabas, 2006)

Messy Church 2, Lucy Moore (Barnabas, 2008)

Footsteps to the Feast, Martyn Payne (Barnabas, 2007)

Children's Bibles

The Barnabas Children's Bible, Rhona Davies (Barnabas, 2007)

Lion Storyteller Bible, Bob Hartman (Lion Hudson, 1995)

Publishers of holiday club and activity session material

BRF/Barnabas: www.barnabasinchurches.org.uk

Scripture Union: www.scriptureunion.org.uk

John Hardwick: www.johnhardwick.org.uk

Kevin Mayhew: www.kevinmayhew.co.uk

Moving schools

It's Your Move (Scripture Union, 2005)

Get Ready Go!, Marjory Francis (Scripture Union, 2002)

Books to display at the occasional offices

The Baptism Cube (Church House Publishing, 2006)

My Baptism Book, Diana Murrie (Church House Publishing, 2006)

Where Did Grandad Go?, Catherine House (Barnabas, 2006)

The Goodbye Boat, Mary Joslin (Lion, 1998)

When Goodbye is For Ever, Lois Rock (Lion, 2004)

Games

For easy-to-organise, cooperative games, the best book is *Instant Games for Children*, Susan L. Lingo (Barnabas, 2009).

*

Notes

How to use this book

1. www.messychurch.org.uk
2. www.isa-gov.org.uk
3. www.ccpas.co.uk
4. www.barnabasinchurches.org.uk

Seasonal activities

1. Search online to find more 'paper angel crafts' and 'egg-carton dragons'.
2. Paper chain links can usually be found in party and birthday shops in the run-up to Christmas, or you can source online.
3. Images of the annunciation can be found through www.textweek.com (click on Art Index). Otherwise, enter 'annunciation' into an internet image search engine.
4. Source 'battery-powered candles' online.
5. To make a Chinese lantern, fold a sheet of A4 paper into half lengthways, and cut a 2cm strip from one of the short sides (to make the handle). Make a series of cuts, about 2cm apart, from the fold to 2cm from the edge, all the way across. Glue the short sides together to form a cylinder. Press down gently so that it bows out in the middle and glue or tape the handle on to the body of the lantern.
6. Search online for adhesive play jewels.
7. To make palm branches from paper, use two sheets of newspaper per person. Roll the newspaper into a loose tube along the short side and tape the roll to hold it together. Make four cuts down from the top of the tube for about a third of the length. Pull up the centre of the tube (from the cut end) to splay out the branches.

8. Wooden crosses can be ordered from www.wooden-crosses.co.uk.
9. *Where is Jesus?* Marjory Francis and Helen Gale (Scripture Union, 2004).

Mission ideas

1. Wooden crosses made from reclaimed wood can be ordered from www.wooden-crosses.co.uk.
2. *A-Cross the World*, Martyn Payne and Betty Pedley (Barnabas, 2004).
3. To find an instructor for a dance event, visit www.idta.co.uk, the International Dance Teachers Association, or look in the local press for adverts from dance schools.
4. *Lion Storyteller Bible*, Bob Hartman (Lion Hudson, 1995).
5. *Better than Halloween*, Nick Harding (Church House Publishing, 2006).
6. The text of the suggested poems can be found by putting each title into an internet search engine. However, please note that some of these poems will be copyright, so further copies should not be made.
7. Tissue paper crowns found in crackers can be bought in bulk from www.fredaldous.co.uk.
8. Small paper carrier bags can be bought from Midpac (www.midpac.co.uk); for paper blowers, visit www.partylily.co.uk; for a picture of a pair of feet, print out a clipart illustration about 4cm square; for a strip of cloth, use 10cm lengths of white tape or plain ribbon; white cottonwool balls are widely available from pharmacies; for party poppers, visit www.partybox.co.uk; cut stars from silver card (craft punches used to press out a star shape in one movement can be purchased from craft shops); for tissue paper crowns, visit www.fredaldous.co.uk; for gold-covered chocolate coins, visit www.chocolatebuttons.co.uk.
9. For tissue paper crowns, visit www.fredaldous.co.uk.

10. To find a template for a square gift box, put 'net of a cube' into an internet search engine. Alternatively, it may be possible to buy cheap, basic gift boxes in the after-Christmas sales.
11. Potters for Peace assists in the production worldwide of low-tech, low-cost, colloidal silver-enhanced ceramic water purifiers. Field experience and clinical test results have shown this filter to effectively eliminate approximately 99.88 per cent of most waterborne disease agents.
12. Kosher sweets can be sourced from www.rumplers.co.uk.
13. Curling ribbon can be obtained from florists and shops that stock birthday goods.
14. Search online to locate icing decorations and wafer decorations.
15. Fibre moulded plates for the Easter Garden competition can be found at www.ripplecups.com.
16. Art images can be found through www.textweek.com (click on Art Index). Otherwise, use an internet image search engine to research 'images of Easter'.
17. Children's pop-up play tunnels, sometimes known as 'wiggle' or 'zig-a-zag' tunnels, can be found through nursery, toy and camping suppliers, www.jacksons-camping.co.uk or www.prezzybox.com.
18. Make-your-own windmill kits can be found at www.bakerross.co.uk.
19. To find instructions for making a paper windmill from scratch, type 'make paper windmill' into an internet search engine. Then scale up the instructions to create a large-scale version.
20. Books about the Holy Spirit include *The Windy Day—Teddy Horsley and the Holy Spirit*, Leslie J. Francis and Nicola M. Slee (NCEC, 1998) and *The Holy Spirit in Me*, Carolyn Nystrom (Moody Press, 1993).
21. Banqueting roll can be bought from catering suppliers such as www.swiftcateringsupplies.co.uk.

22. Licensing arrangements for showing movies can be obtained from Christian Copyright Licensing International: www.ccli.co.uk/licences.
23. Details about the National Association of Child Contact Centres, to locate your nearest Centre, can be found at www.naccc.org.uk.
24. Details of the 'Angel Tree' programme run by the Prison Fellowship can be found at www.prisonfellowship.org.uk. Details of Storybook Dads and Storybook Soldiers can be found at www.storybookdads.co.uk.
25. Wooden key shapes can be ordered from www.wooden-crosses.co.uk.
26. Individuals, as well as groups, can qualify to teach cycling proficiency. Details of the Bikeability award scheme are at www.bikeability.org.uk.
27. Non-Christian organisations that welcome volunteers to help with holidays include Sense for deaf/blind people: www.sense.org.uk; Phab for people with physical disabilities: www.phabengland.org.uk; CHICKS (Country Holidays for Inner-City Kids): www.chicks.org.uk; Children's Adventure Farm Trust: www.childrensadventurefarm.org; Children's Country Holiday Fund: www.childrensholidays.org.uk. All of the above charities also need financial support, as does the Family Holiday Association, which provides breaks for families on very low incomes who have not had a break for more than four years: www.fhaonline.org.uk. The Mothers' Union also works hard to provide holidays for those in desperate need: www.themothersunion.org. Care for the Family also welcome financial support for their lone-parent and child holidays: www.careforthefamily.org.uk.
28. www.wherecanwego.com is a free listing service for events of all kinds.

29. Supplies of cheap printed T-shirts can be ordered from www.vistaprint.com or by searching online for 'custom print T-shirts'. Support Christian companies in this line of work by including 'Christian' in the search request. Make sashes by using 170cm lengths of 10cm wide ribbon, for people to wear diagonally over their shoulder.
30. Divine Inspiration, part of Coventry Diocese: www.divine-inspiration.org.uk.
31. Details of the Backpack Project can be found at www.marysmeals.org. Other charities that support schooling for children in developing countries include World Vision: www.worldvision.org.uk; and Compassion: www.compassion.com. Charities that welcome donations for feeding children include Bible*Lands*: www.biblelands.org.uk; and Save the Children: www.savethechildren.org.uk.

*

Index of ideas

*

General index

Key focus

Key groups

Key Bible verses

Prayer activities

Download materials

About brf:

BRF is a registered charity and also a limited company, and has been in existence since 1922. Through all that we do—producing resources, providing training, working face-to-face with adults and children, and via the web—we work to resource individuals and church communities in their Christian discipleship through the Bible, prayer and worship.

Our Barnabas children's team works with primary schools and churches to help children under 11, and the adults who work with them, to explore Christianity creatively and to bring the Bible alive.

To find out more about BRF and its core activities and ministries, visit:

www.brf.org.uk
www.brfonline.org.uk
www.barnabasinschools.org.uk
www.barnabasinchurches.org.uk
www.messychurch.org.uk
www.foundations21.org.uk

enter

If you have any questions about BRF and our work, please email us at

enquiries@brf.org.uk